ISBN 978-0-331-50941-0
PIBN 11083689

FB &c Ltd, Dalton House, 60 Windsor Avenue, London, SW19 2RR.
Company number 08720141. Registered in England and Wales.

For support please visit www.forgottenbooks.com

requiring the interference of Government." Under the influence of the Ballot Act Stamford returned a Liberal to Parliament, and is so represented to-day, thus overthrowing the ascendancy of the Cecil influence. In connection with this famous election "fight"—for fight it was in very deed—between the scion of the house of Cecil and Charles Tennyson, who was, by the way, an uncle of the present Poet Laureate, the celebrated Stamford "Bull-running" attracted the attention of the country. This "Bull-running," a characteristic example of the rough and often brutal sports of our ancestors, had its origin, so tradition tells, in the time of King John; when one day William, Earl of Warren, standing on the battlements of Stamford Castle, saw two bulls fighting in the adjacent meadows. Some butchers essaying to separate the combatants, one of the infuriated animals rushed into the town, creating a great uproar. The earl, mounting his horse, followed the flying bull, and enjoyed the chase so much that he gave the field in which the battle began to the butchers of Stamford to hold for ever, on condition that they should provide from the rental a bull to be "run" in the town annually on St. Brice's Day (November 13th), the anniversary of the first fight. There is no documentary evidence in support of this tradition, but the town of Stamford undoubtedly hold certain common rights on the spot specified, which is still spoken of as the bull-meadow. The yearly bull-running became an institution of the town; and a Mayor of Stamford, who died in 1756, left a sum of money to encourage the custom. The vestry accounts also show that it was the practice of the church-wardens to give an annual grant towards the sustenance of the "sport." There is an old, and still popular "bullard's" song, which used to be sang at the "running," and at election times when Stamford's distinguishing sport was elevated into a party question, two stanzas of which purport to give the origin of the custom. They run thus:

Earl Warren was the man,
  That first began this gallant sport;
In the castle he did stand
  And saw the bonny bulls that fought.
The butchers with their bull-dogs came,
  [illegible]hose sturdy, stubborn bulls to tame,
But more with madness did inflame;
  Enraged they ran through Stamford.

Delighted with the sport,
  The meadows there he freely gave;
Wh[illegible]hese bonny bulls once fought,
  [illegible]tchers now do hold and have.
By [illegible]er they are strictly bound.
  That every year a bull be found;
Come dight your face, you dirty clown,
  And stump away to Stamford.

It was not until less than a century ago that any attempt was made by the authorities to put a stop to this exciting but brutal entertainment, which was witnessed with much enjoyment by the men of the shires of Lincoln and Northampton. Then the Mayor issued a quaint proclamation, setting forth that bull-running was contrary to religion, law, and nature, and punishable with the penalty of death. The then Earl of Exeter added his influence to the humane efforts of the Chief Magistrate; but the bull was run, and Mayor and earl insulted by the mob. The next year the Mayor, having obtained the assistance of a troop of dragoons to aid him in the exercise of authority, met the bull at St. George's-gate, as it was being driven into the town by the bull woman, a virago jauntily bedecked with streaming ribbons, who played the part of chief matador on these occasions The animal was followed by a crowd of "bullards," as the participators in the sport were styled. On the Mayor appealing to the commander of the cavalry to stop the procession, the dragoon officer declined to interfere, holding that the people were peacefully walking on the highway. "In that case," angrily replied his worship, "your men are of no use here" "Very well," rejoined the officer," "I will dismiss them." The dragoons, on thus receiving their liberty, in great glee joined the "bullards," and the bull was run with more spirit than ever before The townsfolk, delighted with the exciting custom, subscribed to support a second annual bull-running, which, for a time, took place on the Monday succeeding Christmas Day; and there were several occasional supplementary bull runnings, the candidates for the Parliamentary representation of Stamford generally being found ready to give a bull as a means of securing popularity In 1831 the Conservative party canvassed the town under a flag on which a bull was emblazoned. Several clergymen and other humane gentlemen strongly remonstrated against this pandering to a brutal taste, distinctly declaring that they would not vote unless the obnoxious banner were laid aside. But many persons of station defended the practice, declaring that the bull running was "an old-fashioned and manly English sport, inspiring courage, agility, and presence of mind under danger; and as regards humanity, not so cruel to the brute creation, nor so perilous to the life and limb of man as the more generally favoured sport of fox-hunting." Notwithstanding, however, Lord Thomas Cecil fought under the banner of the bull, though he lost the battle. During the polling, and at the hustings, this immense flag, which bore the legend of "A Bull for Ever." was prominently displayed, and made a powerful bid for securing the victory. "A Bull for Ever" was a strange election cry, and as it proved, to the surprise of all, an ineffective one. The struggle between the Marquis of Exeter's nominee and Charles Tennyson is still remembered by the older inhabitants of Stamford, as one of the severest electioneering conflicts ever known in the country. The historian of Stamford tells how the bull was run. About a quarter to eleven on the morning of the festal day, the bell of St. Mary's commenced to toll, by way of warning for the thoroughfares to be cleared of all infirm persons and children. Precisely as the clock struck eleven the bull was turned into a street blocked up at each end by a barricade of waggons. At this moment every post, pump, and coign of vantage was occupied, and those lucky enough to secure such safe positions could grin at their less lucky friends, who had to take refuge in flight, the barricades, windows, and housetops being crowded with excited spectators. The bull, being irritated by all manner of means, was soon worked up into a pitch of fury, and commenced to rush backwards and forwards in wild rage. Then the barricades, being removed, the whole crowd, bull, men, boys, and dogs, ran at full speed through the streets. One great object being to "bridge the bull," the poor beast was, if possible, turned in the direction of the bridge that spans the Welland. The crowd then closing in, with audacious courage, would surround and seize the animal; when, spite of his size and strength, he was hustled by main force over the parapet into the river. Swimming ashore, the bull landed in the meadows, where the "running" was resumed, the miry ground in the wet season about St. Brice's Day, and the falls and other disasters consequent, adding much to the amusement of the mob. This sport was carried on until the poor beast was exhausted, and his tormentors tired out, when he was slaughtered, and the flesh sold at a low rate to the people, who ended the day's carnival with a supper of "bull-beef." Several official attempts were made to put down the barbarous custom, without success, after those already described. In 1839 a stronger force of military and police were sent to Stamford, and every precaution was taken to prevent the bull-running; yet some treacherous special constables smuggled a bull into the town, and the "bullards" had another run. The animal, however, not being at all spirited or formidable, did not afford much sport, and was soon captured by the authorities. In the following year, as bull-running day again drew near, the people of Stamford began to count the cost of their amusement. The military, police from London, and special constables had in two years alone cost the town upwards of £600; a sum which it was wisely thought might with greater fitness have been expended on certain sanitary improvements which were much needed in the borough. So the inhabitants forwarded a memorial to the Home Secretary pledging themselves that if no extraneous force of military or police was brought into the town, they would themselves prevent a repetition of the bull-running. The townsmen were taken at their word, and so the historic custom, which strong measures had so often failed to suppress, was quietly brought to an end. Among the more notable members for Stamford, besides a long roll of Cecils, some of whom were afterwards distinguished by services to the State, may be mentioned Colonel Chaplin, the Marquis of Granby (who subsequently became Duke of Rutland', the Right. Hon. J. C. Herries, Chancellor of the Exchequer under Viscount Goderich, and Sir Frederic Thesiger, First Solicitor and then Attorney-General in Sir Robert Peel's administration, and later Attorney-General under Lord Derby. The sitting member is Mr. M. C. Buzzard, Q.C., who defeated Sir J. C. D. Hay, the Conservative candidate, at the last election, by 60[illegible] votes to 551.

III.—A CLUSTER OF CORNISH BOROUGHS.

THE new allocation of Parliamentary representation will not leave any of the boroughs in the county of Cornwall untouched, but will sweep away from the roll of constituencies all but one. This one—the composite borough of Penryn and Falmouth—preserves its individuality through the action of the first Reform Bill, which joined together the two places for voting purposes, and so brings the number of inhabitants in the constituency above the minimum qualification for possessing one voice at St. Stephen's. Two M.P.'s now sit for the dual borough, but redistribution dooms one honourable member to find his "occupation gone." Though thus the Cornishmen will have henceforth to content themselves with shiral representation, excepting in the solitary surviving borough, there was a time, far back in the good old days, when elections were events which stirred up all the countryside for many a month, when Cornwall played a part in the making up of Parliaments far exceeding in importance that of many a much more densely-populated district. After Grand Councils, sitting irregularly here and there up and down the land at moments of emergency had given place to the beginnings of our present system of fixed Parliaments, there was hardly a town in the tin-mine county but blossomed into a borough, and quickly the representation ran up until two members each were summoned for no less than twenty-seven little places within the confines of the Cornish boundary. This anomaly, which advancing justice has gradually alleviated, now stands within sight of final extinction. Nearly all these petty boroughs owed their birth as such to the circumstance that, in the Plantagenet period, Crown property and power gave the King paramount influence in this corner of his dominion, and, as Wilkes once remarked, the sovereign by inviting every Cornish village to send representatives to the House of Commons, procured a Parliament picked with his own creatures, ready at all times to give effect to his behests. So it was that the first Edward initiated in Cornwall such a system of representation as has had no parallel elsewhere in the kingdom. Not a few of these bogus boroughs, such as Bottreaux Castle, Crofthole, Kilhampton, Millbrook, Padstow, and Polruan, gradually died of inanition; for the burgesses themselves ceased to exercise the franchise from sheer indifference to things of state, or appreciating the burlesque in which they were engaged, surrendered their privilege voluntarily and without regret. Even as near to our time as the passing of the first Reform Bill, however, we find Bodmin, Bossingey, Callington, Camelford, Fowey, Grampound, Helston, Launceston, Liskeard, the two Looes, East and West, Lostwithiel, Newport, Penryn, St. Germans, St. Ives, St. Mawes, St. Michael, Saltash, Tregony, and Truro returning members to Parliament. When qualification began to be considered on the basis of the relative importance of constituencies, of course the bulk of these boroughs soon had their death-knell tolled; and to-day we find but seven of them still in a Parliamentary sense alive. The doom of six of these has now been sounded, as we have already shown. The Cornish boroughs standing on the brink of the grave are Bodmin, Helston, Launceston, Liskeard, St. Ives, and Truro; and it is with these we have chiefly now to deal.

As may well be imagined in such a state of representation as here indicated the electors themselves were far from immaculate. Consulting their own interests, they usually ranged themselves on the side of Mr. "Most," as a Honiton burgess once styled the candidate whose money flowed most freely to Lord Dundonald. The power of the purse and patronage of every kind were the keys wherewith to obtain a Cornish seat. For centuries the franchise was exercised in support of the King's prerogative; and then, step by step, the boroughs became pocket constituencies of peers who had received them as marks of Royal favour. The Earl of Mount-Edgecumbe had the electorates of Bossiney, Fowey, and Lostwithiel at his beck and call; Lord Falmouth's influence was paramount in St. Michael, Tregony, and Truro; the representation of the two boroughs of Looe, which together might make a moderate village, and also of Saltash was controlled by the Bullers. The lord of the manor selected his members, and the dutiful Corporations of his boroughs obediently elected them to sit and legislate as for the constituency. If a patron was away at election times, he would draw up an indenture transferring the control to some one else, and so the system was preserved by deputy. One of the Buller family was once out in India when a contest took place, and relegated his influence to a relative, the then Bishop of Exeter, who duly procured the return of members after his own heart. The "importancy" possessed by mere hamlets was often ridiculous in the extreme, as is amply demonstrated when we remember that the little town of Launceston, together with the insignificant neighbouring Newport, from which it is divided only by a small river, between them had an equal voice in all national affairs with the metropolis itself.

We find Liskeard one of the boroughs which began to return two members as early as 1295, a representation which it enjoyed until the adoption of the first measure of Parliamentary Reform, when it became a single-member constituency. Its electorate formerly consisted of the Mayor and burgesses only; but the £10 householders were duly added, and the limits of the borough extended to the entire parish. Thirty years ago the Liskeard register contained the names of 348 electors, which at the last election had increased to 770, when Mr. Leonard Courtney, the Financial Secretary to the Treasury, and present champion of the Proportional Representation policy, received 370 votes as against 301 recorded for the Right Hon. E. P. Bouverie. A noteworthy incident occurred in connection with Liskeard in 1710. Mr Charles Trelawney had been elected for the borough, but on the meeting of Parliament could not take his seat because the election return was not forthcoming. The Under-Sheriff of Cornwall, being in London, was ordered to attend the House. He explained that the missing document had been stolen by highwaymen. The counterpart of the indenture executed by the Sheriff was admitted as sufficient return, "it appearing to this House that the writ, and the principal part of the aforesaid indenture, were taken away, in coming up to the Clerk of the Crown, by highwaymen, who destroyed the same by burning them." It should be stated that Lord John Russell's 1852 Reform Bill scheduled the two disfranchised boroughs of Fowey and Looe, to be added to the Liskeard constituency. Edward Gibbon, the talented historian of Rome, was returned for Liskeard in 1774, and sat in Parliament for eight sessions. Prudence, he says in his "Autobiography," condemned him to acquiesce in the humble station of a mute. "Timidity was fortified by pride, and even the success of my pen discouraged the trial of my voice." In a letter to a friend he wrote, "I am still a mute; it is more tremendous than I imagined: the great speakers fill me with despair, the bad ones with terror." Again, writing in 178?, describing his life at Lausanne, the then ex-M.P. says: "Acknowledge that such a life is more conducive to happiness than five nights in the week passed in the House of Commons." But elsewhere he says, "I never found my mind more vigorous, nor my composition more happy, than in the winter hurry of society and Parliament." Gibbon supported Lord North's Administration by his vote, and was appointed one of the Lords Commissioners of Trade and Plantations. He was entrusted by Government, at the outbreak of the hostilities with France in 1778, to draw up the official manifesto on that occasion. The following letter is from the historian's correspondence, though, being without date, it does not appear to what nobleman it was addressed: "My Lord,—I am ignorant (as I ought to be) of the present state of our negotiations for peace. I am likewise ignorant how far I may appear qualified to co-operate in this important and salutary work. If, from any advantages of language or local connections, your lordship should think my services might be usefully employed, particularly in any future intercourse with the Court of France, permit me to say that my love of ease and literary leisure shall never stand in competition with the obligations of duty and gratitude which I owe to his Majesty's Government." Gibbon also applied to Lord Thurlow for a diplomatic appointment in 1783, but was unsuccessful. Another parliamentary celebrity, the Right Hon. W. Huskisson, once sat for Liskeard. He commenced his political career in 1792, as secretary to Lord Gower, then English Ambassador in France. He was Under-Secretary for War, and afterwards Secretary to the Treasury, in the Pitt Administration. In 1823 he became President of the Board of Trade, and was greatly distinguished as a political economist, and as one of the earliest advocates of free trade. Huskisson was unfortunate in being at loggerheads with some of his parliamentary contemporaries, and his misunderstanding with the Duke of Wellington was productive of much unpleasantness. But he was a forcible and eloquent speaker, and knew how to give an effective reply in current debate. In some severe remarks in a speech answering an attack by Mr. Williams, the lawyer-member for Lincoln, Huskisson said: "The honourable and learned gentleman repeatedly told us that he was not at liberty to admit this and to admit that. This, I presume, is an expression in which gentlemen of the legal profession are wont to indulge to mark that they keep within the strict limits of their briefs, and that the doctrines which they advocate are those prescribed to them by their instructions. However customary and proper such language may be in courts of law, it certainly sounds new in the mouth of a member of this House." Continuing his defence, the one-time member for Liskeard finally concluded by meeting his opponent's insinuations with "those feelings of utter scorn," to use his own words, "with which I now repel it." Poor Huskisson was killed at the opening of the Liverpool and Manchester Railway in 1830; and just before he died of his injuries, on the evening of the accident, he said, "The country has had the best of me, and I trust it will do justice to my public character."

Truro was created a borough at the same time as Liskeard, and has since had dual representation, the chief influence being in the hands of the Bassett and Falmouth families. The electorate, originally comprising the Mayor and a few select burgesses only, has now increased to a roll of 1561; though, it should be remembered, the population of Truro exceeds 10,000, and the impending loss of both its members by the old borough is considered locally a great hardship. There is a long list of Vivians in the record of members; but the most illustrious representative of Truro was Hammond, the elegiac poet, who was returned in 1741. He made but a poor mark in Parliament, however, and owes his fame chiefly to the fact that his biography is included in the classic "Lives of the Poets." Cibber says Hammond was "inextinguishably amorous," and his mistress "invariably cruel." The poet M.P. cherished an unavailing passion for a Miss Dashwood, and wrote love elegies to unburden his woes. Dr. Johnson thunders against him thus: "Where there is fiction, there is no passion. He that describes himself as a shepherd, and his Nora or Delia as a sheperdess, and talks of goats and lambs, feels no passion." When two local kings shared the ascendancy over a Cornish borough, or the electors preserved a semblance of their freedom and independence, there was often excitement in connection with an election which continued long after the issue had been fought out. The contest was very frequently renewed before the Committee of the House of Commons, and inquiries into election petitions presented from Cornwall very often disclosed much bribery and corruption. But these were the days when every man had his price, and nobody was shocked very much by the evidence adduced. After a famous election for St. Ives, however, in 1775, Mr. Praed, the banker's son, was unseated for bribery. It was shown that large sums of money had been advanced to burgesses on their notes of hand alone. The documents, which were distributed most liberally, purported to be payable with interest on demand at the bank at Truro, but a pretty fair understanding was given that, if the votes were recorded "squarely," the bills would never be called in. St. Ives is one of Edward's favoured boroughs, and we find it returning two members to the first Parliament of "good Queen Bess." It lost a member by the Reform Act, which added the £10 householders, and the voters of Lelant and Towednock to the borough. St. Ives now contains 1037 electors, and is represented by Mr C. C. Ross, who won the seat from the Liberal party on the death of Sir C. Reed in 1881. Its most famous member was the late Lord Lytton, who made his entry into Parliament as representative of St. Ives, in 1831, as Mr. Edward Bulwer. His Reform utterances are matter of history now, but one remark deserves special quotation: "Democracy is like the grave—it never gives back what it receives."

Bodmin, the assize town of the county, returned two members in 1295, and continued to do so until 1867. Lord Vivian's family influence has had the most important control of Bodmin representation. The voters now number nearly one hundred, and the Hon. E Leveson Gower is the sitting member. Noted representatives were Mr. Davies Gilbert, F.R.S., the Right Hon. J. Wilson Croker, many of the Vivians, and Mr. Dum-Gardner, who was elected in 1841, under the pretence that he was Earl of Leicester and oldest son of the Marquis Townshend. Mr. John Wyld, the publisher, was returned in 1857.

Launceston first returned two members at the earliest complete Parliament, one of which it lost in 1832. It has now 868 electors, in whose interests Sir Hardinge Giffard, ex-Solicitor-General, was returned at the last election. The Duke of Northumberland exercises the chief local influence. The great Earl St. Vincent, Mitford, the historian of Greece, Sir John Malcolm, and Admiral Bowles are included among its most important representatives.

Helston, the last on the list of Cornish boroughs, doomed to die, had double representation in the first Edward's days, and was deprived of one by the first Reform Bill. The Duke of Leeds long had ascendancy here, and his interest is still considerable. Mr. W. N. M. St. Aubyn, the Conservative candidate, was returned at the last election, obtaining a majority of forty votes over his Liberal opponent. The register contains at present the names of upwards of 1000 burgesses. Helston has been represented by, *inter alia*, the Right. Hon. C. Abbott, who was Speaker at the commencement of the present century, Lord Bexley (who sat as Mr. Vansittart), Lord James Townshend, Lord Cantilupe, and Mr. Sackville Lane Fox. Helston is singular among constituencies for some of its electoral doings in the days when George the Third was King. The borough had two charters, which left the power of returning members to Parliament in the hands of a Corporation consisting of the Mayor, four aldermen, and an indefinite number of freemen. This curious body had lapsed into such a state of decadence some little time prior to the general election of 1774, that the chief magistrate had ceased to be elected, there was but one alderman, and the Corporation was completed by five burgesses, which imposing confederation made up the entire constituency. The Privy Council made a decree creating a new Corporation with the power of returning two members, which was designed to displace the old moribund council. Under the new charter Mr. Owen and the Marquis of Carmarthen were sent to St. Stephen's; but what remained of the ancient Corporation refused to recognise the altered order of things, and returned Mr. Philip Yorke and Mr. Cust as their members. The result was that the House of Commons recognised the latter, overruled the Privy Council, and ignored the election of the candidates presenting themselves by virtue of its action. When the general election of 1774 followed, the triumphant Corporation had dwindled down to one, a certain Richard Penhall, who combined in his own proper person all that was left of the ancient assembly. Exercising the franchise, he straightway returned the two men of his choice, Mr. Charles Abbot and Mr. Bland Burgess, Under Secretary of State, to represent him in the High Court of Parliament. This essentially single-member constituency went altogether beyond the border land which divides the ridiculous and sublime; and even the tradition revering a House of Commons was, therefore, moved to wipe away such a farce, and adopt the Privy Council's suppressed plan. But old or new Corporation, the influence of the ducal house of Leeds was really always successful and all-powerful in Helston, until the light of the first Reform somewhat impaired its vigour.

THE DYING BOROUGHS.

Episodes from the Parliamentary History of the Towns to be Extinguished by the Redistribution Bill.

BY A FELLOW OF THE ROYAL HISTORICAL SOCIETY.

IV.—MORE OLD BOROUGHS.

MALMESBURY.—WALLINGFORD.—BARNSTAPLE.—LEOMINSTER.

THE birthplace of Hobbes, the philosopher, and William of Malmesbury, is another of those ancient boroughs which have enjoyed a representation in Parliament since the 23rd year of the first Edward's reign. Its constituency originally consisted of the capital burgesses, to whom the first Reform Bill added the £10 householders of the town and suburban district. The family of the Earl of Suffolk, for the time being, have long had chief influence in ruling the political life of Malmesbury. In 1832 the borough had 2 1 electors, while in 1883 the register numbered 1168. Colonel C. W. Miles is the present member, he having been returned in March, 1882, in place of Mr. Powell, deceased. Joseph Addison, the polished poet - essayist, sat for Malmesbury in the House of Commons which was elected in 1708. But, says Lord Macaulay, Parliament was not the field for him; the bashfulness of his nature made his wit and eloquence useless in debate. He once rose, but could not overcome his diffidence, and ever after remained silent. No one will wonder at a great writer failing as a speaker; but many will think it strange that Addison's oratorical failings should have had no unfavourable effect upon his political career. "In our time," proceeds the historian, "a man of high rank and fortune might, though speaking very little, and very ill, hold a considerable post; but it would now be inconceivable that a mere adventurer—a man who, when out of office, must live by his pen - should in a few years become successively Under-Secretary of State, Chief Secretary for Ireland, and finally Secretary of State, without some oratorical talent. Addison, without high birth, and with little property. rose to posts which dukes—the heads of the great houses of Talbot, Russell, and Bentinck—have thought it an honour to fill. Without opening his lips in debate, he grasped a post as high as ever was reached by Chatham or Fox, and this before he had been nine years in Parliament." Truly a career of successful silence, especially when we remember that Addison was as indifferent a Secretary of State as he was a member of the House. He was well-nigh useless to the Government of which he formed a part, from the great difficulty he had in expressing himself intelligibly *viva voce*. Pope says he could not issue an order from his department "without losing his time in quest of fine phrases." When his friend, Sir Richard Steele, stood at the bar of the House defending himself against the charge of having "maliciously insinuated that the Protestant succession in the House of Hanover was in danger," for which offence Steele was expelled from Parliament, Addison stood by his side, and prompted him all through a vigorous, yet unavailing, speech. Lord Wharton's patronage had something to do with Addison's advancement. There is an anecdote of this fluent penman, but notoriously poor public speaker, which will bear repetition here. On a motion before the Irish House of Commons (in which Addison sat as a member for Cavan in 1709), according to Mr. O'Flanaghan, the *littérateur* rose, and having said: "Mr. Speaker, I conceive"—paused, as if frightened at the sound of his own voice. He again commenced—"I conceive, Mr. Speaker"—when he stopped until roused by cries of "Hear! hear!" upon which he once more essayed with "Sir, I conceive——" Power of further utterance was denied, so he sat down admidst the scarce-suppressed laughter of his brother members, which soon burst forth when a witty senator said, "Sir, the honourable gentleman has three times conceived — and brought forth nothing." Charles James Fox, who in the course of his long and brilliant legislative career sat for many boroughs, is the most notable name on the list of past members for Malmesbury.

Wallingford is the oldest of Berkshire boroughs, or at least one of the oldest, for in 1295 we find Reading and Wallingford only sending members from this shire to the Parliament summoned by Edward I. The franchise of the old borough remained unaltered until 1832, when Wallingford was shorn of one member, up to which time the right of returning members was vested in the Mayor, aldermen, burgesses, and inhabitants paying parish rates. The Reform Bill added the £10 householders. The local influence was formerly chiefly exercised by the great legal family of Blackstone. Sir William, the most eminent of his name, himself sat for Wallingford. Besides being the author of the classic commentaries on English law, this celebrated man was a Judge of the Common Pleas, and when he died in 1780 a pension of £400 a year was settled on Lady Blackstone by George III. There are 1241 electors on the register at present, Mr. P. Ralli being their representative. He was returned at a bye election in July, 1880, which took place upon Mr. Wren being unseated on petition.

Barnstaple was one of the old Saxon boroughs, and had a Parliamentary existence as early as the days of Athelstane and his Witenagemote. Since 1295 two members have without interruption been elected by the borough until the present time, when both are to be taken from it. Lord Lymington (who recently married the niece of Sir J. W. Pease, a banker-baronet Friend) and Sir R. W. Carden were returned for Barnstaple at the last General Election. It is remarkable among constituencies for the singular freedom from patronage which its electors have always maintained. Though its choice has not seldom fallen upon a scion of the Fortescue family, Barnstaple stands famous for the independent manner in which its burgesses have exercised the suffrage; and that notwithstanding the representation of the boroughs in Devon and Cornwall has been more under the control of territorial lords than that of any other English district. Its elections have more than once been the subject of enquiry, it is true; but mainly because of this same sturdy refusal to listen to the will of magnates interested in the town who have put forward their own nominees. Barnstaple has returned two famous fighting representatives, Sir Eyre Coote and Lord Exmouth. Sir Eyre Coote took to arms at an early age, and fought against "Bonnie Prince Charlie" in 1745. Nine years later he went to India, and distinguished himself greatly at Pondicherry and elsewhere. The East India Company presented him with a diamond-hilted sword, and made him Commander-in-Chief of their forces. He quitted Madras in 1770, and on arrival in England he was created a Knight of the Bath, and appointed Governor of Fort St. George. Giving himself to legislative work, as member for Barnstaple, he was, of course, regarded as an authority in the House on Indian affairs. But his forte was the field. He was much more at home in camp than council-chamber; and in 1781 he again went East, and with an army of 10,000 men overthrew the rebellious Hyder Ali, whose forces numbered 150,000. The gallant General died in Madras in 1783, and a fine monument to his memory may be seen at Westminster Abbey. Viscount Exmouth is associated with the Devonshire borough by virtue of having been its member in 1802 but his history, like that of General Coote, has much more to tell of shot and shell than speech-making. He distinguished himself as a sea fighter, first coming prominently into notice in connection with the battle of Lake Champlain, in 1776. Rising quickly to post-captain's rank he was in 1793 appointed to command the Nymphe frigate, and after a brilliant engagement captured the French frigate Cleopatra, a piece of service which secured for him a knighthood. After a spell on shore, and a brief representation of Barnstaple, having in the interval received the rank of Rear-Admiral of the Red, the gallant officer was made commander of the East Indian Navy, whereupon he gave up his connection with Parliament. Made Vice-Admiral of the Blue in 1808, he two years later blockaded Flushing, and shortly afterwards was appointed to the Command-in-Chief of the Mediterranean Squadron. Here his tactics in co-operating with the British Fleet on the eastern part of the coast of Spain were marked with conspicuous skill. The value of his services were fittingly recognised in 1814, when he was raised to the peerage as Baron Exmouth of Canonteign, Devon. In the same year he was promoted to the rank of full Admiral, and, subsequently created a K.C.B. and G.C.B. Two years later he was selected to proceed to Algiers to chastise the Dey, for having violated a treaty concluded for the abolition of slavery. His plan of attack was considered by naval authorities as one of the boldest ever attempted by a commander. He entered the harbour with his ship, the *Queen Charlotte*, and, being admirably supported by the other vessels of his fleet, set fire to the Algerine war-ships, bombarded the city, and forced the Dey to yield to all his demands. For this exploit he received the thanks of Parliament, and was made a viscount. Subsequently succeeding Admiral Duckworth in the chief command at Plymouth, he ultimately retired from the service in 1821, and died twelve years later.

Leominster is another of the boroughs born as far back as 1295. Like many other little constituencies its electorate formerly consisted of the capital burgesses, and scot and lot inhabitants, to which the Reform Act added the £10 householders. Its registered electors—779 in 1832—decreased to the extent of over 200 in the twenty years following, but with a widened boundary the borough now numbers a constituency of 864, who are represented by Mr. J. Rankin, who sits on the Conservative side of the House. In the early years of the present century the representation of Leominster was largely at the disposal of the Arkwright family. The present Lord Cranbrook entered the House of Commons as member for Leominster, and sat for the borough from 1856 to 1865, when he took up the representation of Oxford University. Lord Cranbrook, then Mr. G. Gathorne Hardy, son of the member for Bradford, was returned as a Conservative for Leominster upon the death of Mr. Arkwright. Subsequently he rose into prominence in State circles, and occupied the high offices of Under-Secretary of State for the Home Department (1858-59), President Poor Law Board (1866-67), Home Secretary (1867 68), and Secretary of State for War (1874-80), besides being a member of the Council of Education, a Privy Councillor, and a G.C.S.I. Richard Payne Knight, the philologist and writer, sat for Leominster from 1780 to 1784. Knight, who was a Herefordshire man, and inherited much landed property near Ludlow, afterwards sat for the latter borough. At his death he bequeathed his splendid collection of antique art, valued at upwards of £50,000, to the British Museum. Among other notable members for Leominster we may enumerate Rowland Stephenson, the fraudulent banker, Thomas Bish (of lottery renown), Mr. (afterwards Vice Chancellor) Wigram, Lord Hotham (subsequently M.P. for the East Riding of York), and several of the Arkwrights, whose territorial influence here was for some time paramount, as has already been intimated. But the member who reflected the greatest lustre on Leominster was Lord Melbourne, who for some time owed his seat in Parliament to the little western town, now along to be disfranchised. Lord Melbourne was in current debate a most spirited, and sometimes even fiery speaker. Haydon, the painter, who heard him speak on the Irish Church in the Lords in 1833, says, after referring to the calm, deliberative tone of the Duke of Wellington, who had preceded him: "Up starts Melbourne, like an artillery rocket. He began in a fury. His language flowed out like fire; he made such palpable hits that he floored the duke as if he had shot him. But the moment the stimulus was over his habitual apathy got a head; he stammered, hummed and hawed. It was the most piteous exhibition of the night. He waved his white hand with the natural grace of Talma, expanded his broad chest, looked right at his adversary like a handsome lion, and grappled him with the grace of Paris." Viscount Melbourne was Home Secretary in Earl Grey's Administration of 1830-1834. He himself formed Ministries in 1834 and 1835. The first was upset by Peel's Cabinet in the year of its creation; the second lived on for six years. William IV. greatly disliked Lord Melbourne, and the Royal hand was traceable in the summary dismissal of that Minister from office in 1834. When in the succeeding year Lord Melbourne was reinstated in the Premiership after the defeat of Peel, the King could but ill conceal his animosity against his Prime Minister, and occasionally the Royal wrath would break the bounds of courtesy. At a certain Cabinet meeting Lord Melbourne said to his colleagues: "Gentlemen, you may as well know how you stand," and then proceeded to read a memorandum of a conversation between Lord Gosford and the King the day before. His Majesty said, "Mind what you are about in Canada. By —— I will never consent to alienate the Crown lands, nor to make the Council elective. Mind me, my lord, the Cabinet is not my Cabinet; they had better take care, or by —— I will have them impeached. You are a gentleman, I believe. I have no fear of you; but take care what you do." The Ministers present, as we may well imagine, stared at one another, but agreed that it was better to take no notice of what had occurred, and see if the King's excitement would pass away.

THE DYING BOROUGHS.

Episodes from the Parliamentary History of the Towns to be Extinguished by the Redistribution Bill.

BY A FELLOW OF THE ROYAL HISTORICAL SOCIETY.

V.—THE OLDEST CINQUE PORT.

Two of the doomed Parliamentary towns Sandwich and Macclesfield, are in the unenviable position of being partially and wholly disfranchised respectively for corruption at the present moment so that the Redistribution Bill will, in the case of these recalcitrant boroughs but serve to accentuate the sentence of the Bribery Commissioners as passed subsequent to the last General Election. Similar to each other in electoral corruption, they are in one respect as widely different as it is possible for while Sandwich stands on the list of ancient boroughs which has regularly returned two members since 1295, and is in consequence one of the oldest component parts of Imperial Parliament, Macclesfield is one of the youngest born of British constituencies, having only been enfranchised as recently as 1832, under the Reform Act. Adhering to our plan we shall deal with Macclesfield in the final batch of boroughs, proceeding now to speak of some of the associations of its veteran companion in corruption. "Proud Edward"—as Burns styles in his stirring lyric the Plantagenet King who killed the heroic Wallace—summoned two members from the Cinque Port of Sandwich to his sixth Parliament, which was held in the 23rd year of his reign. But Sandwich had been already recognised as a borough thirty years earlier, when, during the long reign of Henry of Winchester, Simon de Montfort, Earl of Leicester, championed the people's cause, overthrew Royal oppression at the Battle of Lewes, and laid down the rude beginnings of popular representation in Parliament in place of what had hitherto been little more than the reigning monarch's ruling council. Leicester's "Mise of Lewes" it was that gave full effect to the Magna Charta which the barons had forced from Henry's father fifty years before at Runnymede. When Henry and his peers and their following of foreigners had to give way before De Montfort and his liberty-loving army of Englishmen, the latter's chief strength sprang from the south eastern and midland counties, London and the Cinque Ports being especially zealous in their adherence to the popular leader. Leicester issued writs to every recognised city, county, and borough, commanding them each to send two representatives to the Parliament which assembled in London on the 2nd of January, 1565. In gratitude for the staunch assistance he had received from the Cinque Ports, the earl directed them to return four members each. But in those early days a borough was an ill-defined and uncertain factor in the State, very much dependent for its recognition or otherwise upon the favour of the rulers of the hour; and Sandwich was not securely grounded as a place possessing indisputable right of Parliamentary representation until 1295, when Edward Longshanks included the ancient and even then thriving town among the burghs of Kent, which the sheriff of the county was commanded to take cognisance of in making up the first really complete English Parliament. Hitherto, the writs had been issued to the local authorities of twenty-one cities and boroughs only, the forty-two members for which, with the four knights of the shire returned by the counties, formed the Parliament; of course, excepting Leicester's irregular summoning of four burgesses each from Sandwich and the other Cinque Ports. Mayors were, however, now ignored, and the shire-sheriffs called on to secure two "discreet" burgesses from no less than 120 different boroughs (and this exclusive of the cities and shires, which latter were now reduced to dual representation) to confer with the King in council at Westminster. A transcript of one of the writs issued by Edward providing for the holding of this memorable assembly will not be here without interest:

"THE KING TO THE SHERIFF OF KENT GREETING.

"BECAUSE we desire to have a conference and treaty with the earls, barons, and other great men of our kingdom, to provide remedies against the dangers the same kingdom is in at this time therefore we have commanded them, that they be with us at Westminster on the next Sunday after the feast of St. Martin, in winter next coming, to treat, ordain, and do, so that those dangers may be prevented.

"WE command and firmly enjoin thee, that without delay thou dost cause to be chosen, and to come to us at the time and place aforesaid, two knights of the county aforesaid; and of every city, two citizens; and of every burgh, two burgesses of the most discreet and fit for business: so as the said knights may have sufficient power for themselves and the community of the county aforesaid; and the said citizens and burgesses may have the same power, separately for themselves and the community of cities and burghs, thus to do in the premises which shall be ordained by the Common Council. So that for defect of such power the business aforesaid may not remain undone; and have then the names of the knights, citizens, and burgesses, and this writ.

"WITNESS the King at Canterbury, the third of October."

Sandwich is the oldest of the Cinque Ports, and was at one time a place of much greater importance than it now is. During the reign of Henry III. it was burned to the ground by the French, but was quickly rebuilt, and made a market town by charter of that monarch. It was a main point of communication with the Continent, and also a rendezvous for the British fleet until about the commencement of the sixteenth century, when the harbour began to fill up, from which time dates the decay of the port.

An earthquake in 1580 completed the destruction of the harbour. The now quiet place, standing four miles from the sea as the river runs, was in the fourth Edward's days a port with ninety-five ships and 1500 sailors of its own, and its Customs yielded £17,000 a year to the revenue. Here Thomas à Becket landed in 1170 on his triumphant return to Canterbury; here Richard the Lion-Hearted set foot on his own soil, after his imprisonment in Austria, twenty-four years later. Edward III. disembarked here after he had capped his victories in France by forcing the citizens of Calais to hand him the keys of their castle and town; and Queen Elizabeth visited Sandwich in 1572, and lodged in a house in Strand-street, which is still shown. In the sixteenth century the town was an abiding place of many French and Flemish refugees, hence the foreign aspect of its bits of ancient architecture. In the Plantagenet period the eminent family of De Sandwich furnished many knights, who held high office in the State: and Henry of that ilk was Bishop of London towards the end of the thirteenth century. The constituency of Sandwich was formerly made up of the freemen of the borough, by birth, service, or marriage, to which body the Reform Act added all the £10 householders. It had a population in 1832 of 12,183, and an electorate of 916; which, in 1883, had advanced to 15,566 and 2178 respectively. The chief influence over the electorate was in the hands of the Lord Warden of the Cinque Ports and the Government of the day. Among the more noteworthy members for the borough may be mentioned Josiah Burchett, who was Secretary to the Admiralty in the reigns of Anne and the two first Georges, and who sat for Sandwich in several parliaments. He was the author of a "Naval History of Great Britain." Admiral Rainier represented the town for a considerable time. Among later members have been Sir E. T. Troubridge, Sir J. R. Carnac, Sir Rufane F. Donkin, Mr C. W. Grenfell, afterwards M.P. for Windsor, and Lord Clarence Paget. Lord Brabourne entered Parliament as Mr. E. H. Knatchbull-Hugessen in 1857, sitting for Sandwich from that time to 1880, when he was transferred to "another place." Prior to his elevation to the Peerage, Lord Brabourne saw service as Lord of the Treasury, 1859-66 Under Secretary for the Home Department, 1866, '69-71; also for the Colonies, 1857-80. Mr. H. A. Brassey and Mr. Knatchbull-Hugessen were returned unopposed for Sandwich in the Liberal interest in 1880; the former still sits for the borough. When the latter was called to the Upper House a contest took place (in May, 1880) for the vacant seat between Sir Julian Goldsmid, who had been rejected at Rochester, and Mr. C H. O. Roberts, who championed the Conservative cause. To the great surprise of all, the latter polled 1145 votes to Sir Julian's 705; but a petition was lodged against Mr. Roberts, and he was unseated. In February, 1881, the Royal Commission which had inquired into the matter reported gross corruption and extensive bribery, the consequence of which we have already shown. Since then the writ in respect of the forfeited seat has been suspended: now both are to be permanently taken away. Sandwich will, however, form the centre of a new county divisional constituency. The Bribery Commission with respect to the Sandwich election cost no less than £2139. One thousand and five persons were reported guilty of corrupt practices. To such a money-making purpose had the franchise in the borough been prostituted that it was proved that 127 of the burgesses had accepted bribes from both sides. One free and independent elector confessed that, such was his interest and integrity in the matter, he tossed up a penny to determine how he should vote, after having first sold it to the friends of both candidates for £3 each. From the Commissioners' report we gather that after dealing with a mass of electoral corruption, that body arrived at the conclusion that taking votes by ballot in Sandwich had not the slightest effect in checking bribery. So general had this giving and taking of material consideration become in the old port, that while the ballot enabled many voters to take bribes on both sides, it did not, as far as the Commissioners could ascertain, render any person unwilling to bribe for fear of bribing in vain. The agent of one candidate, whose expenses were returned at £3153, admitted an outlay of £5600. It will be remembered that a solicitor and a town councillor were sentenced to six months' imprisonment each for active engagement in this wholesale bribing business; and six other offenders in the borough had also to go to gaol for periods of two and three months. These culprits were not afforded the consideration of classification among misdemeanants, the judges remarking that "there was no reason for treating persons convicted of bribery differently from persons who had committed other offences of a bad character." The bribery disclosed here and elsewhere brought about a stringent new measure of electoral law, which is now known as "The Corrupt Practices Act, 1883." There was plenty of evidence to be had that at Sandwich, as in other ancient constituencies, and more especially those largely composed of freemen, the voters had many of them grown accustomed to value their votes at what they would fetch; and that the golden gain of the franchise was an older institution than its penal punishment. The first conviction for bribery did not, according to Hallam, the historian of the Constitution, take place until 1571. Magistrates have since that time been committed to Newgate for the crime of even attempting to bribe, and a certain Mayor of the City of Oxford (which is at this present smarting under a suspended writ for its corrupt propensities), was first imprisoned and then reprimanded on his knees in the House by the Speaker, for seeking to make the most, in a monetary sense, of his position.

Sir Manasseh Lopes, Bart., was mulcted in a sum of £10,000, and sentenced to two years' imprisonment, for bribery within this century; and we might mention many more remarkable instances of a disgraceful system of corruption which has now happily been swept away for ever. Corruption has, however, left a heritage of indelible disgrace to the old Cinque Port of Sandwich.

VI.—ANDOVER AND DEVIZES.

ANDOVER, a borough situated on the skirt of Salisbury Plain, a spot for which antiquaries have claimed identity with the Andaoreon of the Romans, returned burgesses to Parliament as early as 1 95, and continued to be represented for the twelve remaining years of the reign of the first Edward. The regular representation of the borough, however, dates only from Queen Elizabeth's time. We find it sending two members to the fifth Parliament of the virgin Queen, which assembled in 15 6, and from that period to 1867 the dual representation continued without interruption. Then Andover was deprived of its second member. The borough is a place of undoubted antiquity, the Roman road from Winchester to Cirencester having ran directly through it; and several ancient encampments in the near neighbourhood have yielded various objects of archæological interest. That of Bury-hill has been the most extensive and important. The Municipal Corporation was first founded by King John, but the town owes its present charter to the same Sovereign who reinstated it in the list of Parliamentary constituencies—Queen Elizabeth. The fine Gothic church of St. Mary—Andover's chief architectural attraction—has existed since William the Norman's conquest of Britain. In anti-reform days the old constituency was made up of the bailiff and a select number of burgesses. The momentous measure of 1832, which was made law in despite of the determined opposition of the House of Peers, added the £10 householders of the borough and surrounding district, then 323 in number. King William was, as will be remembered, strongly averse to the sweeping Act of Reform, which Earl Grey carried however in the face of Crown and the Upper House. Lord Chief Justice Tenterden's valedictory utterance in Parliament gives us a good illustration of the feeling of the Lords respecting the Act which so affected Andover and the rest of the constituencies, and wrought, in fact, an entire revolution in Parliamentary representation. The peers had exhausted all their powers against the Reform measure, and had at length to bend to the popular will. When the end was seen, Lord Tenterden thus concluded his eloquent assault upon the proposed Act: "This bill, my lords, leaves nothing untouched in the existing state of the elective franchise. It goes to vest all the functions of government in the other House of Parliament; and if it were to pass there would be nothing left for this House, or for the Crown, but to obey the mandate of the Commons. Never—never, my lords, shall I enter the doors of this House after it has become the phantom of its departed greatness." The Lord Chief Justice kept his vow, the Reform Bill received the Royal assent, and the shadow of the great legal peer nevermore darkened the portals of the Upper Chamber. Like Mrs. Partington, a creation of Sydney Smith's witty imagination (and the good dame's celebrity, by the way, dates from this epoch of our history), Lord Tenterden was excellent in overcoming small obstacles, but unequal to interference with a tempest of public opinion stronger than the Atlantic gale which Mrs. Partington—emboldened by her previous successes against slops and puddles—was credited with seeking to subdue with her puny mop at Sidmouth. Andover was, as has been shown, reconstructed as a constituency by this the first Reform Bill, but the electorate rapidly dwindled down from its new eminence. Eighty-one fewer names figured on the burgess roll in 1852 than twenty years earlier; and the voters further decreased to a total of about 200 during the five succeeding years. Then in 1867 Disraeli's Reform Act, which nearly doubled the electors through the country, took away one of the seats from Andover. The electors had been augmented to an aggregate of 866 in 1883; and the population of the borough, 5954 in 1851, remains about numerically the same at the present day. Prior to the passing of the Reform Bill the families of Sir John Pollen and the Earl of Portsmouth had the chief local influence at Andover. Lord John Russell's Reform Bill of 1852 proposed to add to Andover the towns of Basingstoke, Stockbridge, and Whitchurch. Among the members for the borough may be mentioned Sir J. W. Pollen, Mr. Etwall, Lord W. Paget, Mr. H. B. Coles, Alderman and Sheriff Cubitt, the founder of the eminent London building firm, and the Hon. Dudley Fortescue. At the last general election Mr. F. W. Buxton, the banker, was returned in the Liberal interest, the hon. gentleman polling 405 votes against 364 recorded for Colonel H. Wellesley, the Conservative candidate.

Devizes, an important mid-Wiltshire market town, is also a borough of great antiquity, the first charters having been granted by the imperious Queen Matilda, and confirmed by Henry II. Succeeding sovereigns gave new charters and added numerous privileges, of which some are still enjoyed. The existing municipal charter of the town was received from the first Charles. Like Andover, Devizes long had two members, and was deprived of one by the same Act of legislation. The mayor and select burgesses initially formed the Parliamentary constituency, which was increased by the first Reform Bill in the same manner as other then existing boroughs. Devizes has not, for some time, greatly increased its population; but the electorate, 318 in 1832, had risen to 966 in 1883. At the last election Sir T. Bateson, Bart., an ex-Lord of the Treasury, received 446 votes; and Mr. Meysey Thompson, who contested the seat under the Liberal banner, 388. Amoug other historical events of national importance which have occurred at Devizes in earlier times was the imprisonment of Hubert de Burgh, "the gentle *Hubert*" of Shakespeare's "King John," and Prime Minister to Henry III. After his fall he was confined in the castle here, and contrived to escape at night. He took sanctuary at the high altar of the parish church, whence he was forced by the Royal Guards. This act of impiety roused the interference of the Bishop of Salisbury, who excommunicated the soldiers who had thus defied the ordinances of the Church, and desecrated the sanctuary; and the prelate also remonstrated with the King. De Burgh was restored to his ecclesiastical asylum, and though the officers of the Crown and the Sheriff of Wiltshire held the hunted statesman in close siege, with the view of starving him out, by the connivance of two troopers he secretly left Devizes, and was conducted in safety into Wales. Lord Russell's Reform Bill contained a proposal to include Warminster and Heytesbury in the borough, the representation of which was for some time greatly influenced by the local families of Watson Taylor and Estcourt. Since the Reform Act the membership has included Mr. M. Gore, Mr. Locke, Sir P. Durham, Mr. Estcourt, Mr. Jno. Gladstone, Mr. Ludlow-Bruges, Mr. G. and Mr. S. Watson Taylor, father and son, Capt. (afterwards Admiral Sir) J. W. Dean-Dundas, Mr. Heneage, and Mr. C. Darby Griffith. But the most noteworthy representative of Devizes was the Right Hon. Henry Addington, afterwards Viscount Sidmouth, who was chosen Speaker of the House of Commons in 1789, when Pitt was Premier. He was re-elected in 1790 and 1796; and in January, 1801, was chosen to preside over the deliberations of the first House of Commons of our present complete Imperial Parliament, the Act legalising the union of the English and Irish Parliaments having been passed in the preceding July. On the 10th of February following Addington resigned the office of Speaker, and in the course of a few weeks became Prime Minister and Chancellor of the Exchequer. He continued to hold the reins of Government until Pitt's restoration in 1804, and the following year was called to the Upper House. Seven years later he was again in office as Home Secretary under Lord Liverpool. The present Lord Sidmouth, we may here say, in passing, sat for Devizes during 1863-4. A few anecdotes of Speaker Addington's Parliamentary life, before and after his transfer to the "gilded chamber," are not out of place here. The future Lord Sidmouth had just completed his thirty-second year when, on the 8th of June, 1789, he was first elevated to the dignity of Speaker of the House of Commons. In a letter of congratulation upon the event, Mr. Gilpin thus wrote to Addington at the time: "I was in some little pain at first how you could restrain the natural modesty of your disposition on so sudden an elevation to one of the most awful posts I know; but Sir John Dayley and other gentleman gave me such an account of your setting out, that all apprehensions for you are now over; and I have only to regret, as a picturesque man, that such an enlightened countenance as God Almighty has given you should be shrouded in horsehair." The writer had a high opinion of his friend's handsome face thus to deplore that the Speaker's wig should serve to so spoil nature. Addington's abilities have been spoken of as rising to a "respectable mediocrity." Earl Russell says of him: "He was a man of average understanding, equal to the requirements of quiet times, of respectable prejudices, and undoubted courage; but as Minister for a great emergency he excited only ridicule and contempt. Little could he withstand the daily epigrams of Canning, and the scarcely more endurable compassion of Sheridan:

'As London is to Paddington,
So is Pitt to Addington.'

'When his speeches lag most vilely
Cheer him, cheer him, Brother Hiley;
When his speeches vilely lag,
Cheer him, cheer him, Brother Bragge.'

'The Pells for his son, the pills for himself.'"

This latter sally had reference to the sinecure of Clerk of the Pells, and also to Lord Sidmouth's father, who had been of the Esculapian profession, and, in fact, was at one time physician to the elder Pitt. From this circumstance the Speaker derived his nickname of "the Doctor"—a cognomen by which he was frequently called by the satirists of the day. "These and a thousand other arrows which wit squandered upon Addington," says Lord Russell, "utterly ruined him in public opinion." A good story anent Addington's Cabinet, which was certainly not a "Ministry of all the Talents," was related by John Hookham Frere: "I remember old Lord W——, the father of the present lord, a fine specimen of a thorough-going old country Tory, coming to call on my father to tell him that Pitt was out of office, and that Addington had formed a Government. He went through all the members of the new Cabinet, and, rubbing his hands at the end, with an evident sense of relief, said, 'Well, thank God, we have at last got a Ministry without one of those confounded men of genius in it.'" There is an anecdote of Addington and Wilberforce related in the life of the former, which runs as follows: Lord Sidmouth told us one morning at a Cabinet meeting, after an important debate in the House of Commons (the subject of which he had forgotten). Someone said, "I wonder how Wilberforce voted last night." On which Lord Liverpool observed, "I don't know how he voted, but this I am pretty sure of, that, in whatever way he voted, he repents of his vote this morning." Lord Sidmouth added, "It was odd enough that I had no sooner returned to my office than Wilberforce was announced, who said, 'Lord Sidmouth, you will be surprised at the vote I gave last night, and, indeed, I am not myself altogether satisfied with it!' To which he replied, 'My dear Wilberforce, I shall never be surprised at any vote you may give.' Pursuing the conversation, I soon convinced him that he had really voted wrong, when he said, 'Dear, me, I wish I had seen you last night before the debate.'" This incident shows the peculiar fascinating power which Addington was able to exercise, though himself not a man of remarkably strong mind, over characters whose main points were unflinching purpose and iron will. He was more an attractor and cajoler than a leader of men. Lord Sidmouth so ingratiated himself into Royal favour that in Lord Dalling's "Life of Palmerston" we find the author remarking that the necessity of pleasing George III. introduced Addington into so many Administrations as to justify Canning's criticism, "that hewas like the smallpox, that everybody was obliged to have once in their lives." A few days before the declaration of war with France in 1803, a warlike message from the Crown was sent to Parliament. Addington, then Prime Minister, strutted up the floor of the House, bearing this despatch of such imminent moment, in full Windsor uniform, to the amusement of the members, who did not know the contents of the message, and were listening to the Speaker reading an unimportant bill. The burst of laughter which greeted Addington was changed to disgust when he had laid his errand before Parliament. Sheridan, Lord Russell tells us, redoubled the laughter in the House by referring later to the Premier as the right hon. gentleman who had appeared that evening in the character of a sheep in wolf's clothing. Nothing could have been more tragical than the occasion, nothing more farcical than the conduct of the chief actor in the tragedy. Another little story is given by Alison in his "Life of Castlereagh," which will be here *apropos*. At the time of the trial of Queen Caroline (1820), the general excitement roused the popular exasperation against Lords Castlereagh and Sidmouth, the supposed authors of the proceedings, to the highest point; they never appeared in the streets without being hooted and reviled by the mob, and both daily received anonymous letters threatening them with instant death if the bill against her Majesty were not abandoned. They, however, disregarded these threats, and walked about as usual, without any attendants; and the populace, admiring their pluck, abstained from violence. One day they were walking together in Parliament-street, when being recognised, a large mob surrounded them, and they were heartily hooted. "Here we go,'' exclaimed Lord Sidmouth, "the two most popular men in England." "Yes," replied Lord Castlereagh, "through a grateful and admiring multitude."

(To be continued.)

THE DYING BOROUGHS.

Episodes from the Parliamentary History of the Towns to be Extinguished by the Redistribution Bill.

By a Fellow of the Royal Historical Society.

VII. — BRIDPORT. — CHICHESTER. — DORCHESTER.—HORSHAM.—SHAFTESBURY.

The town of Bridport has two claims for distinction: its old renown as the chief seat of the rope-making industry, and its notoriety of to-day as the constituency which furnishes a seat to Mr. Charles N. Warton, that ever-active member of the ourth Party who has attained such celebrity as a "blocker" of bills. At the last election this honourable and learned gentleman secured the representation of the ancient Dorsetshire borough by a ma ority of eight votes only over Mr. P. Ralli, the Liberal candidate, who has since, as we have already shown, been returned for Wallingford. From 1295 to 1867, Bridport exercised the right of sending two representatives to Parliament. Bridport has a place in all dictionaries of English local proverbial sayings, a Bridport dagger being synonymous with a halter. Hence it was once commonly spoken of a person who had been hanged that he had been stabbed with a Bridport dagger; and that the town was famous for the manufacture of good daggers. Ropemaking has for time out of mind been the staple trade of the borough, and was so vigorous in Harry the Eighth's days that the whole of the cordage for the navy was ordered to be made there. Though the town stands on the river Brit, and has a haven and pier, which were restored in the first quarter of last century, the place has never possessed any considerable maritime importance. The old constituency comprised the scot and lot inhabitants, to whom the £10 householders were added in due course, which brought up the electorate to some 500 voters, and these, by subsequent reform measures, have now been rather more than doubled. The most notable members for Bridport have been Lord Hood, Lord Wynford, Sir Evan Nepean, and Sir John Romilly (afterwards Master of the Rolls). Before the Election Petition became a terror to political evil-doers, Bridport was somewhat of a voter's paradise, as in hotly-contested elections as much as £40 has been given and taken for the assistance of a single burgess at the poll. Small as has always been the borough, an election usually cost the candidates, who were usually four in number, almost £2000 each; so that very often the ropefactors had a good time when an appeal to the country was made. The last member which the now dying borough will return has an unenviable notoriety. If he wishes to continue his doubtful assistance in furthering legislation he will have to seek the suffrages of some other constituency at the next general election.

The city of Chichester, like the place last dealt with, had a double membership from 1295 to 1867, and has since returned one member only. The electorate has also been similarly constituted. The register contained 852 names after the first Reform Bill became law, which had decreased to 757 in 1852, though the electors now number some 1300. The Duke of Richmond and Gordon for the time being has long had paramount influence in the representation; and very often a Lennox, as is the case at present, has figured as member for the city. The Rt. Hon. H. C. G. Gordon Lennox, ex-First Commissioner of Works, was returned at the last election by a considerable majority. William Cawley sat for Chichester in the time of the first Charles, and voted for the execution and signed the death warrant of that ill-fated monarch. At the Restoration he, with the rest of the Regicides, had to pay the penalty of persecution. All rawley's large estates round about Chichester were confiscated, and their owner exiled from the country. He died abroad, but his body was privately brought back, and interred on the site of the city poor-house, which he himself founded as an almshouse. In repairing the pavement of this institution, some seventy years ago, the workmen discovered a sepulchral bricked vault in which lay a leaden case, which, it is supposed, contained all that then remained of what was mortal of the one-time M.P. and benefactor of Chichester. The Right Hon. W. Huskisson, the political economist, to whose useful life and sad death we have already had to refer in these papers, sat for Chichester from 1812 to 1823. One of the Smiths, of the eminent banking house of Smith, Payne, and Co., represented the city for a lengthy period. A city and county in its own right, and the scene of several important historical occurrences, Chichester's Parliamentary life has, however, not been an eventful one.

The pretty little town of Dorchester, where the infamous Judge Jefferies held his memorable assize after the Monmouth rebellion in the 17th century, and of which the not altogether impartial historian Clarendon said that no place was more disaffected to the Royalist cause at the time of the great Civil War, commenced its representation in 1295, and lost a member in 1867. The right of election from Edward the Third's time to the passage of the first Reform Bill was vested in the inhabitants paying scot and let, those possessed of real estates within the borough, and those called upon to contribute to the church and poor rates. Then the £10 householders were added, when the burgess roll contained 322 names. Twenty years later these had swelled to 432; and more recent reforms have carried the total number of voters to about 950. Prior to the Conquest, Dorchester was a Crown manor, and after having been conferred upon several Royal favourites in turn, was granted temporarily to the burgesses more than once. Under Henry VI. the grant was made perpetual, and subsequently all the rights and privileges attaching to the manor were vested in the Corporation of the town. The Earl of Shaftesbury and the local families of Sturt and Damer have had much influence in the representation of Dorchester. The present Earl of Shaftesbury — a Christian philanthropist, whose fame is world-wide; but of whom Lord Beaconsfield once spoke as "Gamaliel himself, with the broad phylacteries of faction upon his forehead"—sat in the House of Commons as member for Dorchester. The most important representatives, besides scions of the dominating families, have been Sir Samuel Shepherd, Mr. Richard Brinsley Sheridan (not the brilliant Right Honourable of that name, but his successor), Sir James Graham, and Mr. Williams, the banker. Mr. W. E. Brymer, who defeated Capt. the Hon. F. Greville at the general election by 42 votes in a poll of 706, is the sitting member. Dorchester affords a good illustration of what election petitions were under the old tribunal, when the Court of Inquiry was formed of thirteen members drawn from the House of Commons, who were very often no freer from reproach in the matter of influencing voting than were those upon whom they sat to pronounce judgment. The constituency of Dorchester, as we have said, was formed of those "paying to church and poor" prior to the Reform Act. Under those conditions the famous Dorchester election case was decided. At that time the two members for the borough were virtually returned to the Commons by two members of the Upper House, the Earls of Shaftesbury and Dorchester. A committee declared that an inhabitant need not of necessity be a resident to obtain voting qualification; and that those assessable in respect of real estate within the borough, though neither inhabitants nor occupiers, were entitled to exercise the suffrage. At one election the heir to the earldom of Dorchester had the temerity to stand against his father's interest, and though he obtained two-thirds of the suffrages of the householders, the paternal triumph was not averted, for by a well-managed and carefully-controlled petition the recalcitrant young nobleman was declared not to have been duly elected. Thus hereditary dominance, before Justice had dethroned Favour, generally contrived to obtain its own ends by some method, direct or indirect.

Horsham was created a borough in 1295, and long returned two members. Its representation was reduced to one, however, at an earlier date than any other of the towns alluded to in this chapter. Sir H. Fletcher, Bart., represents the town in the Conservative interest, the voters numbering in the aggregate some 1350. Before the £10 householder received political recognition, the constituency here was made up of all persons having a life interest in the burgage lands and houses. The Howards have always been paramount at Horsham, the Duke of Norfolk being steward of the borough. Many members of the great ducal house have been sent to Parliament by the electors. Lord Surrey, who afterwards in due course was transferred to the Upper House, was returned member for Horsham in 1829, immediately after the passing of the Roman Catholic Relief Act, and was the first of that faith to enter the House of Commons under the new statute. At the same time the then Duke of Norfolk, with two other Roman Catholic peers, took their seats in the House of Lords. The Hon. R. C. Scarlett, afterwards Lord Abinger, also represented the borough. In an election petition presented in 1875 against the return of Mr. Hurst for Horsham, Mr. Justice Field decreed that, even as the law then stood, the payment of a voter's travelling expenses amounted to bribery. It seems that the candidate's agent had written to a voter as follows:—"We find your name on the register. We shall be glad to hear if you will give your support to Mr. Hurst, in which case we shall be glad to pay your travelling expenses." This, the judge ruled (travelling expenses being money within the meaning of the Corrupt Practices Prevention Act of 1854), was an act of bribery both according to the Commons' regulations and the subsequent approval of the House of Lords.

Shaftesbury has also been a constituency notorious for its corruption. It has a representation dating from the first complete Parliament, but was deprived of its second member by the first Reform Bill, which, in adding the £10 householders of the borough to the electorate, included those of Donhead St. Mary, Melbury Abbas, and several other adjoining villages, making a total of 634. The burgesses in 1883 numbered 1372, and returned the Hon. S. C. Glyn as their representative in the Liberal interest. The Marquis of Westminster, Earl Shaftesbury, and the Glyn family divided the patronage of the borough. Among the more noted members have been Sir Home Popham, Mr. Paul Benfield, Sir Charles Wetherell, Lord Howard (the present Earl of Effingham), the Hon. W. B. Portman (M.P. for the county), and Mr. G. B. Matthew. Sir Charles Wetherell distinguished himself by making a strong speech in the House against the Catholic Relief Bill, brought in by the Government, in which he was Attorney-General, and in consequence had to resign. Greville thus writes respecting the speech and the speaker (March, 1829): "The anti-Catholic papers and men lavish the most extravagant encomiums on Wetherell's speech, and call it 'the finest oration ever delivered in the House of Commons;' 'the best since the second Phillipic.' He was drunk, they say. The Speaker remarked that 'the only lucid interval he had was that between his waistcoat and his breeches.' When he speaks he unbuttons his braces, and in his vehement action his breeches work down and his waistcoat runs up, so that there is a great interregnum." At one time the little Dorsetshire town, which is of great antiquity, quite elevated bribery at elections to a fine art, and was the scene of a system of corruption which quite eclipses the illegalities of most other boroughs. The "History of Punch" supplies one of the most dramatic pictures in the annals of Parliamentary contests. The incident belongs to the election of 1774, when Sir Francis Sykes and Sir Thomas Rumbold made a desperate attack upon what in those days was considered to be the private property of Mr. Mortimer. In the course of the trial, which ran on for a month, it was elicited from witnesses that several thousand pounds, in sums of £20 per man, had been distributed among the electors. The candidate's paymasters, who were chiefly the magistrates of the town, hit upon a singular contrivance for use in order to hide, as they thought, where the money came from, or, at any rate, the immediate channel through which it flowed into the pockets of the voters. A person dressed up in representation of our old friend "Punch," and called by his name, was placed in a small apartment, and through a hole in the door delivered out to the voters parcels containing the twenty pounds. They were then conducted into another apartment of the same house, where they found a person called "Mr. Punch's secretary," and here went through the farce of signing notes of indebtedness for the "value received," but which were made payable to an imaginary character to whom they gave the curious designation of "Glenbucket." Two witnesses, called by the counsel for the petitioner, swore they had seen "Punch" through the hole in the doors, and that they knew him to be a certain Mr. Matthews, well known as an agent for one of the sitting members. The committee who unseated the members added to their decision an instruction to the House of Commons that the most notorious bribery and corruption had prevailed at the election in question, and recommended the withholding of the issue of a new writ for the borough until a fuller inquiry could be instituted. Notwithstanding all the thunders of Parliamentary Committees, however, the representation of Shaftesbury went on, and the custom of receiving a substantial consideration for the "favour of vote and interest" came to be looked upon by the burgesses as a sort of prescriptive right. Shaftesbury in later days has evinced a surprising independence of all political discrimination, disregarding the consideration of the questions dividing Liberal and Tory, and dutifully returning the nominee or favourite of the patron of the borough for the time being. But of course open bribery has had to be refrained from; and the emoluments of the freemen who once existed mainly upon the price obtained by trafficking away their birthright have been reduced to the vanishing-point.

(To be continued.)

THE DYING BOROUGHS.

Episodes from the Parliamentary History of the Towns to be Extinguished by the Redistribution Bill.

By a Fellow of the Royal Historical Society.

VIII.—THE LAST OF THE OLDER BOROUGHS.

There are still some dozen boroughs to be dealt with which can point to a representation dating from A.D. 1295. These ancient constituencies we purpose to dispose of—necessarily with brevity—in the present paper. Lewes returned two members from the time of the earliest complete Parliament to the passing of the Reform Bill of 1867, when one was taken away. The burgess-roll contained first the names of scot and lot inhabitants, then the "ten-pounders" were added, and finally the householders. The electors in 1832 numbered 872, but these decreased during the next twenty years to 713, largely through the death of freemen of the borough. Under the new order of things, the burgesses in 1883 amounted in the aggregate to 1483, who are now represented by Mr. W. L. Christie. The political patronage of Lewes has for time out of mind vested mainly in the Pelhams, whose dominance was occasionally, however, shared by the Blunts. Old Nicholas Pelham lies entombed in St. Michael's Churchyard, Lewes, his memorial stone inscribed with the punning epitaph:

> "What time the French sought to have sack't Sea-foord,
> This Pelham did re-pel 'em back aboord."

The family did much service in guarding the Sussex coast in Plantagenet and Tudor days, and therefrom derived much political power, which has continued down to this present; the Earl of Chichester's influence being still very considerable. Lewes is a town of great county importance, and was of some celebrity even before the Conquest. Among eminent members who have sat for Lewes may be mentioned Viscount Hampden, who owed his seat to the borough—when plain Right Hon. H. B. W. Brand—from 1852 to 1868. He was Secretary to the Treasury for some seven years, and twelve years filled with distinction the Speaker's chair. A former member for Lewes, the Right Hon. Henry Fitzroy, a scion of the ducal house of Grafton, who was for some time Speaker Brand's colleague in the representation of the town, narrowly missed being elected to preside over the deliberations of Parliament. He held office as Under-Secretary for the Home Department, and Lord of the Admiralty; and was Chairman of Committees. During the Speakership of Mr. Lefevre, he for some time acted as deputy in that gentleman's absence from the House through illness. Sir James Scarlett, (afterwards Lord Abinger), Sir Howard Elphinstone, Lord Cantelupe, and Philip York are also noticeable names on the list of members; and this latter is the most illustrious of them all. He was elected for Lewes in 1718; and after serving with honour, first as Solicitor and afterwards Attorney-General, was in 1733 made Chief Justice of the King's Bench, and raised to the peerage, He was a most eminent luminary of the law, and besides being Sir Robert Walpole's right-hand supporter, enjoyed the esteem of the nation for his high judicial integrity and attainments. In 1736 he was created Lord Chancellor, an office which he fulfilled for twenty years; and in 1754, he was advanced to the Earldom of Hardwicke.

The borough of Cockermouth returned members in the first Edward's days, but discontinued the exercise of its electoral privilege for nearly a century and a half, not sending representatives regularly again until 1640. From then to 1867 two members were sent to the Commons by the Cumberland borough *Sans* interruption, when one was struck off by the hand of Reform. The franchise was formerly limited to the burgage tenants only, and the electors, 305 in number in 1832, are now over 1000. Mr. Edward Waugh is the sitting member. The house of Egremont has exercised much influence in the borough in time past. General Wyndham, the then representative of this family, himself sat for Cockermouth some thirty years ago, and his nephew, Lord Naas (Lord Derby's Irish Secretary,), was returned by the burgesses in 1857. The first Earl Stanhope, Lord Macartney, the Earl of Liverpool, and Lord Abinger are among the most celebrated of Cockermouth's past representatives.

Calne has not much to entitle it to note except its antiquity. It has been a single-member constituency since 1295, and has long had the reputation of being a pocket borough of the Marquis of Lansdowne, and is to-day represented by a member of his lordship's family in the person of the Under-Secretary for Foreign Affairs, Lord Edmund Fitzmaurice. The influence of the marquis has presumably preserved Calne from extinction hitherto, for it is among the least important in point of population of the dying boroughs. Before the £10 householder became a political factor, Calne's electorate was composed of the burgesses of the borough only. In 1832 there were 519 names on the roll; these dwindled down to little more than 200; but since household suffrage has been inaugurated the list has swelled to an aggregate of 993 electors. Lord Russell's Reform scheme proposed to increase the constituency of Calne by adding the parish of Melksham. In the "good old times" the borough counted among its members John Dunning (the celebrated Lord Ashburton), and Colonel Barré (one of the many notabilities to whom the authorship of "Junius" was attributed). A long array of Fitzmaurices have sat for Calne, and the gallant Sir William Fenwick Williams, of Kars, was returned for the borough in 1857.

Cricklade first returned two members in 1295, and has maintained the dual representation to this date, though the borough was temporarily disfranchised for two years—1780-82—for gross bribery. The constituency, in ante-Reform days, was made up of the freeholders and copyholders of the burgage houses and holders of three years' leases. After the bribery proceedings, just over a century ago, this limited and, as the evidence showed, corrupted electorate was deprived of its exclusive privilege, and was extended by adding several adjoining parishes to an aggregate of about 1200. The constituency grew to a total of 1534 in 1832, and 1647 a quarter of a century later; and there are now about 8000 burgesses. Professor Story Maskelyne and Sir Daniel Gooch are the present members for Cricklade. The Earl of Carnarvon's influence was considerable here at one time. None of the representatives call for special mention.

Bridgnorth was deprived of one member in 1867, and had previously returned two from 1295. The first Reform Bill changed the constituency from the freemen, resident and non-resident, into the resident freemen and £10 householders, making a total of some 750, which has since increased to 1218. The old Shropshire families of Pigot and Whitmore have had much to do in decreeing the representation, and several members of both have sat for the borough. It is notable that a Whitmore was M.P. for Bridgnorth during the Long Parliament, and 230 years afterwards the family's influence was still so great that another of the same name fulfilled the same honourable position. The present Lord Acton was member for Bridgnorth from 1865 to 1869. Mr. W. H. Foster, Deputy-Lieutenant for the County, is the sitting member.

Wilton, to which old borough the county of Wilts owes its name, was a place of note long anterior to the Conquest, and returned two members from 1295 to the passing of the Reform Bill of 1832, when one was taken away. The Earl of Pembroke, whose palatial residence here is memorable as the place in which Sir Philip Sidney composed his "Arcadia," has long had chief influence over the electorate, and the heir to the earldom, the Hon. S. Herbert, is the sitting member. At the last election Mr. Joseph Arch contested the seat, but only succeeded in polling 397 votes, against his powerful opponent's 818. There are at present over 1400 electors. Before the first Reform Bill the Corporation and burgesses only formed the constituency. Among the most noted members for Wilton were the then Mr. Henry Lytton Bulwer, and the first Earl of Malmesbury, the great diplomatist, who sat as Mr. Harris. The present Earl of Malmesbury represented Wilton in 1841. He has twice held the important offices of Foreign Secretary and Lord Privy Seal.

Chippenham was in the time of Alfred the Great one of the finest towns in Britain. A borough by prescription it returned two members to the earliest complete Parliament. In the first year of the reign of Mary it was incorporated by charter. James I. granted a new charter to the freemen and burgesses. The Parliamentary life of Chippenham as a two-member constituency continued till 1867, when one was withdrawn. Sir G. Goldney, Bart., is the sitting member.

he having defeated Mr. S. Butler at the last election by 23 votes. The electors number over a thousand. The great Sir Robert Peel sat for Chippenham from 1812 to 1817. The wealthy Neeld family had paramount influence in the representation.

One of the smallest of existing boroughs, Evesham, returned two members from 1295 to 1867, and has since sent one only. At the last general election Mr. D. R. Ratcliffe was returned by a majority of nine votes over his Conservative opponent, but was unseated on petition. A new election in July of the same year further showed how evenly-balanced parties are in the borough. Mr. F. Lehmann, fighting in the Liberal interest, received 378 votes, and Mr. F. D. D. Hartland, the Conservative candidate, had 376 recorded in his favour. Another petition ensued, and one vote being struck off the latter's number, and six off the former's, Mr. Dixon Hartland was left in a majority of 3. The burgesses and freemen were the old electorate. The Rushout family dominated the local influence for a very considerable period, and the head of the house, the present Lord Northwick, sat for Evesham from 1837 to 1847 as Captain Rushout. Subsequently representing East Worcestershire, he succeeded to the title in 1859. Among other members for Evesham have been Lord Marcus Hill, Sir C. Cockerell, Sir H. P. Willoughby, and Mr. Grenville Berkeley.

Lymington, a borough in the reign of the first Edward, returned two members down to 1867. The Corporation and freemen formed the old electorate. When the first Reform Act added the £10 householders the constituency numbered 249. These had increased in 1857 to 338, and the number of electors is now 817, who are represented by Colonel E. H. Kennard. The aged Earl of Albemarle, born in 1799, and still surviving, sat for Lymington for twenty-three years as Colonel Keppel, being first returned in 1832. The Burrard family were chiefly masters of the political situation in the borough for a lengthy period. Among others, Sir John Rivett Carnac, Sir Harry Burrard-Neale, and the historian Gibbon have been returned as members for the ancient Hampshire port.

Guildford first returned two members in 1295, and was deprived of one by the Reform Act of 1867. The constituency originally consisted of the freemen and scot and lot freeholders, to whom the great change of 1832 added the £10 householders of the ancient borough, together with those of the outlying parishes of St. Nicholas and Stoke, bringing up the electorate to a total of 342. These were increased during the twenty years immediately following to 648, and the burgesses now number 1542, whose chosen representative is Mr. Denzil R. Onslow, late of the Indian Government service. Earl Onslow and Lord Grantley have enjoyed chief influence as to the representation, and for many years the two noble families shared the seats between them. Sir Fletcher Norton, Speaker from 1768 to 1782, was member for Guildford. In a memorable Land Tax debate, which took place before the Christmas recess of 1770, shortly after an unseemly discussion had occurred in the Lords, some honourable members were growing clamorous, when the Speaker interposed, to quote the *Public Advertiser*, "with all the softness of a bassoon," with the deliverance, "Pray, gentlemen, be orderly; you are almost as bad as the other House." But Sir Fletcher Norton had little right to inveigh against impetuosity of speech. Ten years after the above occurrence he descended to the floor of the House, and took part with much warmth in a current debate, he expressing himself in strong antagonism to the increasing influence of the Crown, and making an unmeasured attack upon the policy of Lord North. He had previously distinguished himself by deliberately flouting the King in taking up a bill from the Commons to the Lords, which granted his Majesty an augmentation of income for the payment of his debts. Mr. Serjeant Best, afterwards Lord Wynford, and another light of the law, and the father of a family of eminent lawyers, Mr. William Bovill, Q.C., were both indebted to Guildford for seats in Parliament, as was also Major (afterwards Sir John) Yorke Searlett.

The grand old historic town of Warwick has had uninterrupted dual membership from the first complete Parliament to the present time, and now, after such a lengthy existence as a borough, and with the Speaker of the House of Commons as its senior sitting member, it is doomed to early effacement from the list of places entitled to separate representation. The Earls of Warwick have had chief influence in the constituency right up to the days when justice and right banished patronage and political domineering. Many a Greville has been associated in the part with the representation. Mr. Speaker Peel's colleague in the membership for Warwick is Mr. George William John Repton, grandson of Lord Chancellor Eldon, who was first returned for the borough 33 years ago, having previously sat for St. Albans when that city had its voice in the making up of Parliament. The scot and lot inhabitants anciently formed the constituency. In 1832 the addition of the £10 householders increased the electorate to 501, and further reforms have carried the voters' list to an aggregate of about 1800. The most noteworthy members, apart from immediate connections of the Earl of Warwick, and the present representatives, have been Sir C. E. Douglas, the Hon. C. J. (afterwards Lord) Canning, and Mr. Edward Greaves, the local banker.

Shoreham, now an adjunct of Brighton, with a population of over 42,000 inhabitants, has had independent dual representation from 1295. First formed of the scot and lot freeholders, the constituency was increased in 1771 to the 40s. freeholders of the whole Rape or Hundred of Bramber, to whom were subsequently added the "ten-pounders," and in due course the householders. The most noteworthy incident in the Parliamentary life of this borough is that connected with the "Christians," a local club identified with electoral corruption. In 1771, so flagrant had electoral misdoings in the old shore borough become, that the matter formed subject for enquiry in the House of Commons. It had been discovered that the "Christians," an association of freemen professedly banded together for the furtherance of charity, were exercising their functions in reality in negotiating the sale of the representation to the highest bidder. This was done by the agency of a secret committee, which concluded a transaction with the most liberal candidate, received the money, and divided the spoil among the club generally. As the members of this committee abstained from voting themselves, "on the ground of conscientious scruples," they escaped the imputation of bribery until a disagreement with the returning-officer, who was in their confidence, led that functionary to reveal their plans. It appeared that at this particular election there were five candidates, two only of whom came anything near the "Christian Society's" expectations with their offers. General Smith bid £3000, and would further undertake to benefit the township by building shipping there. Mr. Rumbold offered £35 a vote all round to every freeman, and this tempting bait won the allegiance of the body. The General, however, stood first with the returning-officer, and the disagreement led to a public quarrel. The Opposition of the day wished to disfranchise Shoreham, but were out-voted, the House resolving that some eighty-one of these curious Christians should never be received at the poll again, and that the boundary of the borough be extended to cover a much wider area. Sir W. W. Burrell and Mr. R. Loder are the last members for Shoreham.

IX.—MORE PLANTAGENET BOROUGHS.

We have now dealt with the whole of the boroughs of eldest birth—that is, those which can clearly trace an electoral life dating from the first complete Parliament, which assembled in 1295. Fourteen more constituencies returned representatives later in the Plantagenet period, and these next claim attention.

Hertford's status, as a borough, dates as far back as 1298, when two members were first returned. This representation continued until the 7th year of the reign of Henry V., when the bailiff and burgesses petitioned to be relieved from the burden of sending members on the score of poverty. The request was granted, and an interregnum occurs in the representation reaching to the closing year of the first Stuart sovereign's occupation of the English throne, when the elective franchise was restored. Two members were again regularly chosen until 1867, when Hertford was shorn of its second representative. The electorate formerly consisted of the freemen and inhabitants not in receipt of parish relief. The population at the passing of the first Reform Bill was 5247, thirty years later it had increased to 6605, and at the last census the number returned was 8556. There were 700 electors in 1832, and the burgess roll after the lapse of half a century contained the names of 1112 voters, who are now represented by Mr. A. J. Balfour, who sits on the Conservative side of the House. Earl Cowper and the Marquis of Salisbury were [illegible] of the chief local influence. Earl Stanhope (then Lord Mahon) and Lord Ingestre (afterwards Earl Talbot and Shrewsbury) were returned for Hertford in 1832, but were unseated on a bribery petition, and no new writ was issued for the borough until the general election of three years later, which re-established the Melbourne Ministry in power. One of the members returned on this occasion was the Right Hon. W. F. Cowper, stepson of Lord Palmerston, and nephew of Viscount Melbourne, whose private secretary he had for some time been. Among other State offices filled by this scion of the Cowper family were those of Under Secretary for the Home Department, Vice-President of the Council of Education, Lord of the Treasury, and of the Admiralty. Other notable members for Hertford were Sir W. M. Townshend Farquhar, Bart., and Mr. T. Chambers, the latter of whom achieved some celebrity for his vigorous crusade against the Maynooth grant and conventual institutions generally.

Wycombe first returned two members A.D. 1300, and the dual representation was maintained until the passing of the Disraeli Reform Bill. The electorate, anciently composed of the Corporation of Freemen, was increased by the addition of the £10 householders in 1832 to a total of 298, which has now multiplied so greatly that there are over 2000 voters, and the borough boasts a population of upwards of 13,000. Colonel Gerard Smith is the sitting member, he having been elected in 1883 to fill the vacancy caused by the retirement of the Hon. Colonel Carington, heir to the baronage of his own name. The present lord sat for Wycombe from 1865 to 1868. Lord Beaconsfield made his earliest attempts to enter Parliament as candidate for Wycombe, but unsuccessfully wooed the suffrage of the electors, though he had the advantage of recommendation from Hume and O'Connell. The influence of the Caringtons, Fitzmaurices, Dashwoods, and Barings, has been considerable here. The great Lord Shelburne (afterwards first Marquis of Lansdowne), who succeeded Lord Rockingham as Premier, and made young William Pitt his Chancellor of the Exchequer, was the most celebrated Fitzmaurice who has sat for Wycombe. He had to complain that the borough, despite the family interest, was in his time a costly one to contest, as much as £700 being paid for a single vote. Corruption seems to have raged rampant in Wycombe in the bad old days. The election of 1725 is noteworthy for the issue of a false return by the Mayor, who manipulated the votes polled to give his own favourite, Mr. Collyer, a majority of one. This audacious result was, however, upset by the House of Commons. Here the "chairing" of members is said to have originated, Wycombe having enjoyed the reputation of metropolis of chair-making. Colonel Jervis, afterwards Earl St. Vincent, the naval hero, represented the borough, as did also the third Earl Stanhope, Ralph Bernal Osborne, the "Stormy Petrel of Debate;" and, not least notable, John Archdale, the first "Friend" who ever sat in the Commons, who was returned in 1698, considerably over a [illegible] to the election of Mr. [illegible] that the matter formed subject for enquiry in the House of Commons. It had been discovered that the "Christians," an association of freemen professedly banded together for the furtherance of charity, were exercising their functions in reality in negotiating the sale of the representation to the highest bidder. This was done by the agency of a secret committee, which concluded a transaction with the most liberal candidate, received the money, and divided the spoil among the club generally. As the members of this committee abstained from voting themselves, "on the ground of conscientious scruples," they escaped the imputation of bribery until a disagreement with the returning-officer, who was in their confidence, led that functionary to reveal their plans. It appeared that at this particular election there were five candidates, two only of whom came anything near the "Christian Society's" expectations with their offers. General Smith bid £3000, and would further undertake to benefit the township by building shipping there. Mr. Rumbold offered £35 a vote all round to every freeman, and this tempting bait won the allegiance of the body. The General, however, stood first with the returning-officer, and the disagreement led to a public quarrel. The Opposition of the day wished to disfranchise Shoreham, but were out-voted, the House resolving that some eighty-one of these curious Christians should never be received at the poll again, and that the boundary of the borough be extended to cover a much wider area. Sir W. W. Burrell and Mr. R. Loder are the last members for Shoreham.

IX.—MORE PLANTAGENET BOROUGHS.

We have now dealt with the whole of the boroughs of eldest birth—that is, those which can clearly trace an electoral life dating from the first complete Parliament, which assembled in 1295. Fourteen more constituencies returned representatives later in the Plantagenet period, and these next claim attention.

Hertford's status, as a borough, dates as far back as 1298, when two members were first returned. This representation continued until the 7th year of the reign of Henry V., when the bailiff and burgesses petitioned to be relieved from the burden of sending members on the score of poverty. The request was granted, and an interregnum occurs in the representation reaching to the closing year of the first Stuart sovereign's occupation of the English throne, when the elective franchise was restored. Two members were again regularly chosen until 1867, when Hertford was shorn of its second representative. The electorate formerly consisted of the freemen and inhabitants not in receipt of parish relief. The population at the passing of the first Reform Bill was 5247, thirty years later it had increased to 6605, and at the last census the number returned was 8556. There were 700 electors in 1832, and the burgess roll after the lapse of half a century contained the names of 1112 voters, who are now represented by Mr. A. J. Balfour, who sits on the Conservative side of the House. Earl Cowper and the Marquis of Salisbury were long possessed of the chief local influence. Earl Stanhope (then Lord Mahon) and Lord Ingestre (afterwards Earl Talbot and Shrewsbury) were returned for Hertford in 1832, but were unseated on a bribery petition, and no new writ was issued for the borough until the general election of three years later, which re-established the Melbourne Ministry in power. One of the members returned on this occasion was the Right Hon. W. F. Cowper, stepson of Lord Palmerston, and nephew of Viscount Melbourne, whose private secretary he had for some time been. Among other State offices filled by this scion of the Cowper family were those of Under Secretary for the Home Department, Vice-President of the Council of Education, Lord of the Treasury, and of the Admiralty. Other notable members for Hertford were Sir W. M. Townshend Farquhar, Bart., and Mr. T. Chambers, the latter of whom achieved some celebrity for his vigorous crusade against the Maynooth grant and conventual institutions generally.

Wycombe first returned two members A.D. 1300, and the dual representation was maintained until the passing of the Disraeli Reform Bill. The electorate, anciently composed of the Corporation of Freemen, was increased by the addition of the £10 householders in 1832 to a total of 298, which has now multiplied so greatly that there are over 2000 voters, and the borough boasts a population of upwards of 13,000. Colonel Gerard Smith is the sitting member, he having been elected in 1883 to fill the vacancy caused by the retirement of the Hon. Colonel Carington, heir to the baronage of his own name. The present lord sat for Wycombe from 1865 to 1868. Lord Beaconsfield made his earliest attempts to enter Parliament as candidate for Wycombe, but unsuccessfully wooed the suffrage of the electors, though he had the advantage of recommendation from Hume and O'Connell. The influence of the Caringtons, Fitzmaurices, Dashwoods, and Barings, has been considerable here. The great Lord Shelburne (afterwards first Marquis of Lansdowne), who succeeded Lord Rockingham as Premier, and made young William Pitt his Chancellor of the Exchequer, was the most celebrated Fitzmaurice who has sat for Wycombe. He had to complain that the borough, despite the family interest, was in his time a costly one to contest, as much as £700 being paid for a single vote. Corruption seems to have raged rampant in Wycombe in the bad old days. The election of 1725 is noteworthy for the issue of a false return by the Mayor, who manipulated the votes polled to give his own favourite, Mr. Collyer, a majority of one. This audacious result was, however, upset by the House of Commons. Here the "chairing" of members is said to have originated, Wycombe having enjoyed the reputation of metropolis of chair-making. Colonel Jervis, afterwards Earl St. Vincent, the naval hero, represented the borough, as did also the third Earl Stanhope, Ralph Bernal Osborne, the "Stormy Petrel of Debate;" and, not least notable, John Archdale, the first "Friend" who ever sat in the Commons, who was returned in 1698, considerably over a century prior to the election of Mr. Pease (for South Durham), who is often spoken of as the earliest Quaker member. Col. Barré, to whom we have already had to refer, was M.P. for Wycombe in 1761. He, on Lord Mayor Crosby and Alderman Oliver being committed to the Tower for arresting messengers who had taken citizens of London into custody for breach of parliamentary privilege in 1771, denounced the conduct of the House as infamous, and adding that "No honest man could sit amongst its members," left his seat, and walked away. "Parliament," writes Horace Walpole, "were obliged to swallow so ungrateful a bolus."

The city of Lichfield returned two members in 1305, and continued to exercise the privilege occasionally during the two succeeding reigns, after which there seems to have been an apathetic feeling towards the franchise until 1552, when the representation was resumed and maintained as at first until 1867, from which date the city ceased to be a two-member constituency. The present member, Col. T. J. Levett was returned at an extraordinary election in July, 1880, which arose out of the unseating of Col. Dyott on petition, the latter having defeated Sir J. Swinburne, the Liberal candidate, by a narrow majority at the general election. Sir John again contested the seat with Col. Levett, and ran him also closely on the poll. There are 1243 electors, out of a population of 8360, in the city, according to the latest returns before us; the numbers having been 861 and 6499 respectively at the passing of the first Reform Bill. The ancient constituency comprised the magistrates, freeholders, burgage-tenants, and scot-and-lot inhabitants. The Earl of Lichfield and the Duke of Sutherland have had paramount political power in the city. Lichfield's claims to consideration as a place of historical note arise more from its civic and ecclesiastical associations than its Parliamentary connection. The present Earl of Harrowby was M.P. for Lichfield from 1856 to 1859, and the Earl of Lichfield sat for the city from 1847 to 1854. Other eminent names associated with the representation of the constituency include those of Lords Waterpark, Paget, Granville, Mostyn, and Wrottesley.

Midhurst, which commenced to return two members in 1311, and was deprived of one by the first Reform Bill, has only 1136 electors and a population of 7277 according to the latest returns accessible; and had as few as 250 voters even after its second member was taken away and the franchise extended. The little Sussex constituency was regarded as a pocket borough of the Percivals, Earls of Egmont. It has narrowly escaped political extinction previously, and indeed was only saved by enlarging the boundaries in 1832. Before the Reform Bill, the electorate consisted of the burgage tenants only, within living memory but 120 in number. One Lord Montagu, then owner of Midhurst, had occasion to dismantle some of these burgage tenements, in order to widen the limit of Coudray Park; but he was careful to have stones placed in the new wall, indicating the site of each ancient burgage, whereupon a certain noble duke is credited with having remarked that the elective franchise had fallen so low at Midhurst that the very stones appeared as voters for Parliament. Midhurst gave Charles James Fox a seat in the House of Commons when he was but a lad of nineteen, and that in his absence from England. Chief Justice Pratt, Lord Plunket, Earl Stanhope (as Lord Mahon), Earl Spencer (then Capt. F. Spencer), Sir Horace B. Seymour, the Right Hon. Spencer H. Walpole (three times Lord Derby's Home Secretary), and the present Earl of Egmont are among the most illustrious members for Midhurst. Samuel Warren, the author of "Ten Thousand a Year," "The Diary of a Late Physician," and some other noteworthy books, a barrister of considerable celebrity, was returned for the borough in 1857. Midhurst, which, we may take it, has hitherto been allowed to retain an unwarranted share in political affairs "only as a peace-offering to the House of Lords," to quote an utterance of the Irish statesman Shiel concerning the borough, is at present represented by Sir H. T. Holland, Bart., K.C.M.G., an ex-Under Secretary for the Colonies.

Weymouth has sent two members since 1315, and two more for its suburb of Melcombe Regis from 1319; but the two were united by the Reform Act of 1832. The constituency was originally composed of the corporation, freemen, and freeholders, and a very small "stake" seems to have sufficed to give title to the franchise. Oldfield relates that "a committee was appointed to try the petition of one John Arbuthnot on the 10th February, 1804, against the return of certain candidates for the borough. In consequence of the decision of this committee two hundred freeholds were at once split into two thousand. Freeholders of Weymouth were to be found in London, and in almost all the towns and villages to the Land's End, as also in the Channel Islands, whence many hundreds were afterwards brought at great expense to vote at every election for the borough. Some even voted for the thirteenth hundredth part of a sixpenny freehold." At one time, says a writer on this borough, Weymouth's "local influence was a matter of purchase," but it was in the hands of the famous "Bubb Doddington" in his day. He himself sat for Weymouth, and he afterwards took the title of Lord Melcomb from the adjacent borough, which was one with Weymouth for municipal purposes as early as the reign of Queen Anne. Afterwards the Johnstone family obtained political ascendancy here, and several of them sat for the borough. A list of the chief names of note among the representatives of Weymouth gives those of Sir Christopher Wren, Joseph Hume, Sir T. Fowell Buxton, Lord Villiers, Sir E. Sugden (afterwards Lord St. Leonards), and Col. Freeston, who served with distinction in the Peninsular War. Sir Walter Earle, who was member for the borough in 1641, has had his memory kept alive by reason of a protest he made against note-taking in the House. Sir Thomas Fowell Buxton, who fought in the forefront of the battle for freeing the negro slave, was returned for Weymouth in 1818, after a very severe contest, in which seven candidates went to the poll. He kept his seat in Parliament for nearly twenty years, during which period he did much good and philanthropic public work. Of more recent members we may mention the Earl of Wilton, who sat for Weymouth from 1859 to 1865. The sitting members are Sir F. J. W. Johnstone, Bart., and Mr. Henry Edwards. The strength of the electorate in 1883 was 1771 in a population of 13,704.

Maldon enjoyed dual representation from 1329 to 1867, when one member was taken away and the other left. The Essex market borough claims some distinction as the spot on which Edward the Elder encamped in A.D. 913, for the purpose of impeding the progress of the invading Danes, and traces of an intrenchment are still discoverable. Prior to the passing of the Reform Act, which added the £10 householders, Maldon's burgess roll contained the names of freemen of the town only. "Borough-English," a law which provided for the succession of the youngest son at his father's death, has been exemplified at Maldon in connection with the burgage tenements. A charter, *temp.* Henry II., provided for the local government of the borough by a mayor, four aldermen, and twelve councillors. The population, 4895 in 1832, rose during the next twenty years to 5888, and now stands at considerably over 7000; while the voters, who numbered 716 when the first Reform Bill was passed, and 845 in 1857, now total 1481. Mr. Geo. Courtauld, sitting in the Liberal interest, was returned at the last general election by a majority of eighteen votes over his Conservative opponent, Sir W. N. Abdy. During the last half century the names of Mr. Quintin Dick, Mr. T. B. Lennard, Mr. Peacocke, Mr. Bramley-Moore, and Mr. Thos. Western, besides Mr. Du Cane (afterwards member for the Southern Division of the County), Mr. John Miller, who was unseated on petition, and elected later for Colchester, and Mr. David Waddington, who subsequently sat for Harwich, have occurred as those of representatives for Maldon.

Until the passing of the first Reform Bill, Wareham returned two members to Parliament—a privilege which it began to exercise in 1329. One was struck off, and the single representation has survived until the present time; there being now rather more than 1100 electors, and a population of about 6200. The magistrates, scot-and-lot inhabitants, and occupying freeholders were the constituency before the Reform enlarged it by statutory additions; the effect of the earliest measure being to bring the voters' list up to 387, which further increased to 418 in the following twenty years without alteration in the qualification for the franchise. Mr. M. J. Guest was returned at the general election under the Liberal banner, to the discomfiture of Mr. J. S. W. Drax, the representative of an influential local family. The Draxes, Bankes, and Calcrafts have mainly enjoyed political ascendancy at Wareham of late years. Sir Samuel Romilly, the eminent lawyer and reformer of the criminal code, who ultimately brought a busy and useful life to a sorrowful close by his own hand when reason had left him after the loss of his wife, sat for Wareham during part of his Parliamentary career. "Single-speech Hamilton" is also claimed by Wareham as a celebrated representative. He was Secretary to Lord Halifax, George the Third's first Lord-Lieutenant. His first measure was a proposal to raise six regiments of Irish Roman Catholics, amounting to 3000 men, to be taken into the pay of Portugal, then our ally. The proposal was made in a lengthy and eloquent speech; but the matter roused such Protestant Opposition that the Government abandoned the bill. This famous speech was delivered in 1755. Walpole tells us that Hamilton "broke out like the Irish rebellion, three score thousand strong, when nobody was aware, or in the least expected it." Another notable member for Wareham was Lord Denman, who was returned in 1818; and was afterwards appointed Solicitor and Attorney-General, and ultimately Chief Justice of the Queen's Bench. His defence of Queen Caroline gained him much popularity.

MORE PLANTAGENET BOROUGHS.—

(Continued)

Tavistock, an old borough by prescription, regularly returned two members to Parliament from 1331 to 1867, when the representation was reduced to one. The town seems to have risen from the monastic house here, which was once so important an establishment that its abbot had a seat in the House of Peers. John Peryn, the last of the abbots of Tavistock, surrendered the building and its belongings to the Crown in 1539; and King Henry bestowed the ecclesiastical house and estate, together with the borough, upon John, Lord Russell, ancestor of the Duke of Bedford, the present noble proprietor. By the disfranchisement of Tavistock, the ducal family loses what has been well described as the securest piece of parliamentary patronage in the kingdom; for ever since the dissolution of monasteries a Russell, or a nominee of the Russells, has sat for the borough. The present member, Lord Arthur Russell, brother to the Duke of Bedford, has represented Tavistock since 1857. There are 937 electors on the roll, which, up to the passing of the first Reform Bill, contained the names of the freeholders only. Among members for the borough we may mention the late Marquis of Tavistock, the late Sir R. J. Phillimore, the eminent judge of the Court of Arches and of the Admiralty Court (who was M.P. for the Duke of Bedford's town from 1853-7), and the present Viscount Enfield, who was the latter's colleague in the representation. Lord Enfield (who sits in the Upper House as Baron Strafford) has seen service as Parliamentary Secretary to the Poor-law Board, Under Secretary for Foreign Affairs, and Under Secretary for India. General Fox also figures among the representatives; but the most noteworthy member for Tavistock was the patriotic John Pym, who was returned for the picturesque old Devonshire borough in the reign of James I. What a thorn in the side of his Stuart sovereign he afterwards became is notorious, for among the bold figures of that stirring time of civil strife, few stand out more prominently than that of the irrepressible "King" Pym, as he came to be called by his contemporaries. He sprang from an old Somerset family, and was a Calvinist of the sturdiest type. He championed the cause of the Commons as against the Crown and the peers, defying all the powers of the nobility, and setting the King at naught. Pym had a leading part in the impeachment of Buckingham and Strafford; he made a violent speech in attack upon Archbishop Laud; and it was his impetuosity, perhaps, more than all else, which brought the ill-fated Charles Stuart into the House of Commons to seize in his rage the famous five members, of whom Pym was chief, who opposed the Royal will. The erstwhile member for Tavistock continued firm in his allegiance to the Parliamentary party up to his death, but did not live to see the terrible consequences of the revolution which his fiery and unflinching spirit did so much to bring about. He was a man of many parts, shrewd and discerning, and possessed much of the power of moving men to action by eloquent words. Pym was laid to rest with great solemnity in Westminster Abbey.

Beaumaris, the chief place in the Isle of Anglesea, which owes its present importance to its beautiful situation, has been a single-member constituency since 1356. The first Reform Bill, in adding the £10 householders to the electorate, formerly composed of the Mayor, bailiffs, and capital burgesses only, also greatly enlarged the boundaries of the borough, bringing within radius Holyhead, Almwich, and Llangefni. The voters in 1832 numbered only 329, now there are over 2500 on the register. Mr. Morgan Lloyd, Q.C., was returned at the last general election without a contest for Beaumaris, and has represented the borough since 1874. His predecessor was the Hon. W. O. Stanley, who sat for Beaumaris some seventeen years, having previously represented Chester and Anglesey. The chief local influence was exercised by the noble house of Pagets, Marquises of Anglesey and Earls of Uxbridge. A member of the family represented Beaumaris from the passing of Earl Grey's Reform Bill to the return of the Hon. W. O. Stanley. Queen Elizabeth re-incorporated Beaumaris in the 4th year of her reign. The first Edward placed a fortress here, after he had erected the castles of Conway and Caernarvon; but little of historical note has taken place in the now favourite North Welsh resort.

The borough and Cinque Port of Rye enjoyed dual representation from 1369 to 1832; and the Reform Bill, in taking away one member, added Winchelsea to the constituency. It had then acquired an unenviable reputation for bribery and corruption. It was disclosed in evidence that at one election Sir Frederick Dashwood paid as much as £30 to each of those who voted for him. The gallant candidate also gave a handsome present to the wives and daughters of the freemen. Shortly before the commencement of the present century the proprietors of Winchelsea effected a sale of their property to one Nesbitt, he paying £15,000 for his purchase. Greatly to the annoyance of the burgesses they were not taken into account at all in the matter. The *largesse* they were accustomed to receive at every election was not made known at the time of transfer to Mr. Nesbitt; but that gentleman was quickly informed that unless the same handsome treatment of the freemen as had hitherto obtained were not continued, the Parliamentary privileges that he would enjoy in connection with his acquisition would be but limited. With the fusion of Rye and Winchelsea, corruption did not become altogether a thing of the past; for we find Mr. Jeremiah Smith, who had much political influence here, was convicted of bribery in 1852. There are now 1387 electors, who are represented by Mr. F. A. Inderwick, Q.C. The names of "Bubb" Doddington, Lord Liverpool, the Duke of Wellington, and several of the Curteis family occur in the list of members. The Curteises have had a large share in the Parliamentary patronage since Reform Bill times.

Westbury was enfranchised by Henry VI. in 1449, and returned two members until the passing of the first Reform Bill. It has, with an enlarged franchise, only just over 1000 electors. Mr. C. N. P. Phipps was returned to the doomed remaining seat at the last election. The Lopes family, several of whom have represented Westbury, had political preponderance for a lengthy period there. Sir William Blackstone was also member for the little constituency. Westbury has not had a pure electoral life. A petition in 1869 showed that a local manufacturer had exacted a promise from his workpeople that they would abstain from recording their votes in an election in which a rival manufacturer was one of the candidates. This strong partisan went so far as to announce, even at such a recent date, that no man should remain in his employment who voted for the man of his dislike. Professor Prym records that he had seen Westbury not only advertised for sale, but offered by order of the Court of Chancery. Tierney, an election agent, told Sir Samuel Romilly (*vide* the latter's diary, *anno* 1807) that he offered £10,000 for the two seats at Westbury, then under Lord Abingdon's control, but offered in vain. In 1571 a fine was imposed on the borough for receiving a bribe from one Thomas Long, "being a simple man and of small capacity to serve for Westbury." The mayor was ordered to repay the money, though Long does not seem to have been expelled. This, according to Hallam, is the earliest recorded instance of punishment for electoral bribery. Long made some disparaging public utterances respecting the Queen, for which he was, by order of Elizabeth's Council, set in the pillory at Cheapside.

Poole maintained its double membership from 1455 to 1867, when one was struck off. The old ante-Reform constituency was composed of the Corporation and freemen only. There are now more than 2000 electors within the bounds of the parliamentary borough. Mr. C. Shreiber defeated Mr. C. Waring by six votes only at the last general election;

and on the death of Mr. Shreiber, Mr. W. J. Harris was returned in 1884. The contests have often been very close in this borough. Charles James Fox, in 1775, presented a petition against the return of a Mr. Manger and General Sir Eyre Coote for Poole. Fox contended that the inhabitants, a majority of whose votes had been recorded in his favour, were the real electorate, and the "commonalty" meant in the charter of the borough. The committee of enquiry decreed, however, that "commonalty" properly signified corporation, and as the municipal magnates and their followers had supported the General and Mr. Manger, these were held to be duly elected. A seat was secured for Poole by imprisoning a burgess for debt at one election. Mr. Sturt and Mr. Taylor would have polled the same number of votes, but one of the last-named gentlemen's supporters was taken into custody at the entrance to the polling-booth, and offer of bail or payment of the amount due absolutely refused. The friends of Mr. C. Waring were so indiscreet in their zeal for his return in 1874 that that gentleman was unseated for corrupt practices on the part of his agents. A singular subterfuge was resorted to. The election expenses were remarkably small; but the expenses *after the event* proved the reverse. £479 was returned as total cost, but it was proved in evidence that bills to the amount of over £1300 were paid for refreshments, &c., immediately after the struggle, and these were said to have been dispensed subsequently.

The two last of the Plantagenet boroughs are the towns of Ludlow and Wenlock. The former commenced to regularly return two members in 1473, the latter five years later. Wenlock, by far the larger of the two Shropshire constituencies, retains the dual membership until the time of writing; Ludlow lost one in the Reform Act of 1867. The old agricultural market town of Wenlock returned Messrs. A. H. Brown and C. T. W. Forester as its representatives at the general election, and has some 3365 voters in a population of upwards of 20,000. The Earl of Bradford and Baron Forester have had chief influence over the Parliamentary representation; and the present Lord Forester himself sat for the borough from 1828 to 1874, when he succeeded to the title. He was Comptroller of the Royal Household under Lord Derby's *régime*. Mr. J. Milnes Gaskell, a Lord of the Treasury in Sir Robert Peel's day, was for some time Lord Forester's colleague in the representation of Wenlock. Col. the Hon. G. H. W. Clive, returned in 1880 for Ludlow, first became member for that borough twenty years earlier. The old constituency, before the enfranchisement of the £10 householders, was made up of the resident common-burgesses, together with their sons and sons-in-law; the electors, numbering 359 in 1832, increased to 450 during the succeeding twenty years, and now reach over a thousand. The Earl of Powis had the principal part in the political patronage, and several of the Clives, before the present member, have been indebted to this circumstance for their seats in Parliament. Mr. R. Payne Knight, of classical celebrity, and Mr. Botfield,

F.S.A., F.L.S., and a member of other learned societies, represented Ludlow at different periods. The history of the town is intimately associated with that of its grand old castle, the habitation of the Lords Presidents of Wales, who there held the Court of the Marches. Butler there, too, wrote part of his "Hudibras," he being then steward of the castle; and from thence Milton's "Comus" was given to the world. But with the many notable historical events which have occurred, purely in connection with the fortress, we have nothing to do here.

XI.—SOME TUDOR CONSTITUENCIES.

The Border borough of Berwick has had regular representation by two members since the reign of Henry VIII., having previously sent one member only to the Scotch burgh-court. Anterior to its obtainance of a recognized position as a constituent part of the English Parliament, Berwick had been called upon to send members in the time of Edward IV. The electorate originally comprised all the burgesses and freemen, resident or not; but, with the enlargement of the franchise in 1832, the non-residents were struck off the register. In adding the £10 householders the first Reform Bill widened the bounds of the constituency, taking in the voters of two adjoining townships. Among prominent members for the borough may be mentioned the first Lord Minto and General Sir R. Donkin. Another notable representative, was Lord Barrington, an Irish viscount, who was expelled from the House of Commons in 1728 for "promoting, abetting, and carrying on the fraudulent undertaking called the Harburgh lottery." From Lord Waldegrave's "Memoirs" we gather that Henry Fox, writing to Lord Hartington on the subject of the Berwick election of 1754, at which the celebrated John Wilkes, although unsuccessful, spent between £3000 and £4000, gave the following interesting information: "Mr. Wilkes, a friend it seems of Pitt's, petitioned against the younger Delaval, chosen at Berwick, on account of bribery only. Delaval made a speech on his being thus attacked, full of wit, humour, and buffoonery, which kept the House in a continued roar of laughter. Mr. Pitt came down from the gallery, and took it up in his highest tone of dignity. He was astonished when he heard what had been the occasion of their mirth. Was the dignity of the House of Commons on such sure foundations that they might venture themselves to shake it? Had it not, on the contrary, been diminishing, by sure gradations, for years, till now they were brought to the very brink of the precipice, where, if ever, a stand must be made?" In 1880 Berwick returned Sir D. C. Marjoribanks and the Hon. H. Strutt as its representatives. The latter succeeded to the peerage of his father, the first Baron Belper, a few months later, and the next year the former also was called to the Upper House as Lord Tweedmouth. On the first vacancy a close contest ensued, Colonel Milne-Home defeating the Right Hon. J. M'Laren by two votes only; and Mr. H. E. H. Jerningham was elected in the October of 1881 in the seat given up by Baron Tweedmouth. The latest return gives the electorate as numbering 2145.

Petersfield first returned two members to Parliament in 1532, but was deprived of one by the first Reform Act. The constituency formerly consisted of the freeholders of certain lands within the ancient borough limits, to which were added in 1832 the £10 householders of Petersfield and seven other tithings. The registered electors have risen from 234 in 1832 to 353 twenty years later, and a present aggregate of 864. The principal influence over the representation at one time rested with the Jolliffe family; but the Hon. W. S. H. Jolliffe, who sat from 1874 to 1880, was then defeated by Mr. W. Nicholson, the Liberal candidate. His father, Sir W. G. Hylton Jolliffe, who represented Petersfield both before and after the passing of the first Reform Bill, was Under-Secretary for the Home Department for Lord Derby in 1852, and received a call to the Upper House as Baron Hylton in 1866 on the "Rupert of Debate" succeeding for the last time to the Premiership. Other notable names among the members for Petersfield are those of one of the Dukes of Portland, Lord Wynford, Mr. Canning, and Mr. J. G. Shaw-Lefevre (father of the Postmaster-General), who was afterwards knighted and made a K.C.B. He served with distinction as Clerk of the Parliaments, and was, it may be mentioned, brother to Viscount Eversley, who so long and honourably presided over the deliberations of the House of Commons.

In 1536, memorable for the passing of the Act suppressing monasteries, the counties and certain towns in Wales, together with the county and city of Chester, were admitted to Parliamentary representation. This alteration added thirty members to the House of Commons, including the member for Calais. Brecon, Cardigan, Haverfordwest, and Radnor, which then had their birth as Parliamentary boroughs, we have now to deal with, as having been included in the fatal "Schedule I." of the new Seats Bill. Brecon, or more properly Brecknock, the capital of the county, has some 878 electors, who returned Mr. Cyril Flower as their representative at the last general election. The old constituency of the Corporation and free burgesses was enlarged in 1832 to include the £10 householders of the town, and of Castle-hill and Christ's College. Some years ago the political influence was divided between the local families of Morgan (now Barons Tredegar) and Watkins. Colonel Lloyd Vaughan Watkins, then Lord-Lieutenant of the county, was returned in support of Lord Palmerston in 1857. The town has many interesting historic memories, which we cannot here refer to. Cardigan, with its connected neighbouring towns, Aberystwith, Adpar and Lampeter, has now an electorate of 2160, and a population reaching 14,500. Mr. David Davies, the colliery proprietor, was returned unopposed at the general election. Prior to the Reform Act, the freemen formed the constituency exclusively. The Earl of Lisburne and the Pryse family have had the leading influence with the electors. Lord Kensington, Comptroller of the Royal Household, and a former Groom-in-Waiting to her Majesty, has represented Haverfordwest since 1868. Here the Philipps family were long paramount, and Sir R. Bulkelly Philipps (afterwards Lord Milford), was one of the members for the borough. The old constituency of Haverfordwest, with which were included for Parliamentary purposes St. David's, Fishguard, and Narberth, was composed of the freeholders, burgesses, and scot-and-lot inhabitants. There are 1495 electors on the roll, as against 723 in 1832 and 682 in 1851. Enlarged franchise measures have increased the voters, while the population has rather fallen off in numbers during the last half-century in the picturesque Pembrokeshire county town. The Radnor district of burghs, five in number previous to 1832, had Presteign added by the Reform Act. Lord Hartington was returned for this constituency in 1880, as well as for North-East Lancashire, and he, electing to sit for the county, Mr. S. C. E. Williams was chosen in his stead. The latter retired in October of 1884, and Mr. C. C. Rogers was selected to succeed him without opposition. There are 917 voters on the roll, and a population of 6700, which shows a considerable decrease within living memory. The local families of Price and Lewis have had much to do with the representation. Robert Harley, first Earl of Oxford, and his son, the collector of the celebrated Harlean MSS., are among the more noted members for the constituency; and we may mention also Philip Warwick, who distinguished himself in the "Grand Remonstrance" debate of 1641; and the Right Hon. Sir T. Frankland Lewis, Bart., who was succeeded in 1855 in the membership by his more distinguished son, Sir George Cornwall Lewis. The latter held many high offices of State, and also earned much fame in the world of literature as an author and critic while editor of the *Edinburgh Review*.

Though Buckingham was summoned to send two members to Parliament as early as 1295, it does not seem to have complied until 1542, and from the reign of Edward VI. regularly returned two representatives until 1867, when one was struck off. The great ducal house of Buckingham has largely dominated the Parliamentary interest of the borough; indeed, some member of the Grenville family sat for Buckingham for nearly two centuries, and the present duke was M.P. for the constituency at an early period in his distinguished career. Sir Harry Verney was first returned to Parliament by the Buckingham burgesses in 1832, and, besides having since sat for Bedford, has several times been again chosen member for Buckingham, the last occasion being the general election of 1880. There are now some 1103 electors, but prior to 1832 the constituency was formed of the bailiff and twelve burgesses. Sir Edmund Verney, the First Charles's standard bearer at Edgehill, was member for Buckingham in 1623, and Browne Willis, the antiquary, in 1705. Other noteworthy representatives were Francis, (eldest son of that Sir Richard Ingoldsby who married Oliver Cromwell's aunt), who sat during the Protectorate, and had the good fortune to be well received at Court after the Restoration; Dr. Radcliffe, founder of the Radcliffe library at Oxford; the great Earl of Chatham; besides several successive Grenvilles and Temples who made their mark in history. Buckingham is a place of great antiquity, but was enumerated among the decayed cities and towns for the relief of which an Act of Parliament was passed in Henry the Eighth's reign; and in a charter granted to Buckingham by Queen Mary in 1554 it is especially provided that "the stay of the representatives at the Parliament shall be at the cost and charges of the borough and parish and the community of the same."

Next comes a batch of boroughs, the regular representation of which dates from the first year of the first Queen Regnant of England. The three Yorkshire towns of Thirsk, Knaresborough, and Ripon, together with Banbury and Aylesbury, present themselves for notice in this connection. With regard to the constituencies situated in the "many-acred shire" there is much of great interest that space prevents us from recounting. Ripon city especially teems with old-time incident. The Studley Royal estate passed successively from the families of Le Gras, Tempest, and Mallory, into the hands of John Aislabie, of South Sea Bubble renown. He was member for Ripon in 1720, and Chancellor of the Exchequer. He, with several other members of Parliament, was expelled from the House for participation in this gigantic financial fraud. Aislabie, it was said, made over a quarter of a million profit by his transactions in the stock of the Company, and out of his gains probably obtained the wherewithal for laying out the magnificent gardens at Studley, and the purchase of Fountain Abbey. The Chancellor was sent to the Tower, and ordered to refund the sums he had so unlawfully gathered together. The Allansons and the Lawrences succeeded to the ownership of Studley and its princely belongings; and some forty years ago Mrs. Lawrence bequeathed the famous property to Earl de Grey, since which time the Robinsons have reigned in Ripon. The ex-Viceroy of India's little Yorkshire city's present and last representative, the Right Hon. G. J. Goschen, is among the most distinguished of its members. Ripon enjoyed dual representation until 1867. The burgage-holders, prior to the introduction of a systematic qualification for the franchise, were here, as in many other Yorkshire boroughs, the voters at Parliamentary elections, and often found their privilege a lucrative one. Thirsk lost its second member by the action of the first Reform Bill. It was long a close borough in the hands of the Frankland-Russell family, and several of the Franklands have sat in Parliament by virtue of the connection, but at the general election, when the Hon. L. P. Dawnay was returned, Sir W. A. Frankland was placed ignominiously at the bottom of the poll; while Major Stapylton ran the successful candidate rather closely. Thirsk has fewer voters and inhabitants than Ripon, the numbers being: Thirsk, 968 and 6306; and Ripon, 1112 and 7390. The Dukes of Devonshire have wielded the political power in the quaint old-world looking Nidd-side market town of Knaresborough, which kept the right of returning two members until 1867, and now loses its remaining representative, Colonel Gunter, who was only returned recently on the death of Mr. "Tom" Collins. Knaresborough, which is the very least of the dying constituencies, with 728 voters only and a population of 5000, has numbered among its members Sir James Mackintosh, the Right Hon. G. Tierney, and Lord Brougham. The burgesses in old days had not here a high reputation for political purity, and their descendants can scarcely claim exemption from reproach, for the 1882 Bribery Commission cost them some £2258. Stapleton, the biographer of Canning, says: I remember Canning's being very much amused when (having to deal with Knaresborough, then a close borough in which the Duke of Devonshire's interest was paramount, and for which Tierney and Sir J. Mackintosh were the members), he discovered the following sentence in a publication describing the borough: "The members never appear at the elections, and it is the constant practice to chair two old paupers by way of proxies." His merriment was unbounded at the idea of such grave old members of Parliament having those undignified representatives on these important occasions. Banbury has never been more than a single-member constituency; and at one time its electorate consisted only of the eighteen members of the ancient Corporation. There are now, however, 1874 burgesses by reason of reform measures, and Sir B. Samuelson, the ironmaster-baronet, is its representative. The celebrated Frederick Lord North, Premier "when George III. was King," was member for Banbury, and his family had considerable local influence. Frederick Douglas, Lady Glenbervail's son, sat in Parliament for the then family borough of Banbury, and amused us one day, says Harford, in his "Recollections of Wilberforce," by telling what had formerly occurred to some recreant electors, who had ventured, though vainly, to oppose Lord North's nomination of the mayor. Shortly before the annual dinner, to which his lordship was in the habit of sending venison, the old steward, while carving it, sent plenty of fat to the obedient voters, but made the rebels feelingly sensible of his displeasure by exclaiming, as he despatched their respective plates, "Those who didn't vote for my lord's mayor sha'n't have none of my lord's fat." Aylesbury will retain its dual representation until the Seats Bill takes effect, Sir N. M. de Rothschild and Mr. G. W. E. Russell, Secretary to the Local Government Board, having the present care of the Parliamentary interests of the important constituency of some 29,000 inhabitants and about 4500 burgesses. Of old, the electorate was formed of the mayor, aldermen, and twelve burgesses, to whom succeeded the lords of the manor, who were in turn superseded by the "pot-wallopers" of the borough not in receipt of alms. Gross bribery being brought to light at Aylesbury in 1804, the forty-shilling freeholders of the adjoining hundreds were added to the constituency. The patronage of the representation was formerly entirely in the hands of the Duke of Buckingham. John Wilkes, who was expelled the House in 1764 for his outspoken advocacy of the liberties of the people, Lord Lake, the celebrated Indian General, the graceful poet Praed, Lord Nugent, the apostle of the ballot, Mr. Layard, of Nineveh renown, and in the interregnum, Thomas Scott and Simon Mayne, the regicides, have been returned members for Aylesbury, but the demand of space prevent us enlarging on these and other interesting associations of the borough.

(To be continued.)

XII.—SOME TUDOR CONSTITUENCIES (*Continued*).

DROITWICH first returned a member to Parliament in 1554. Its consituency anterior to the Reform Bill was a very close one, consisting of the Corporation of Salt-springs only; and the representation was largely dominated by the Pakington and Foley families. Sir John Pakington, Colonial Secretary to Lord Derby, in later life Secretary for War, and ultimately raised to the peerage as Baron Hampton, sat for Droitwich for many years. The electors (now numbering 1410), chose at the last general election Mr. J. Corbett, the salt-mine proprietor, as their representative. Abingdon, as Sensham and the Abbey-town of early times, was a place of much importance, and the theatre of many Saxon Parliaments, but was regularly recognised as a place entitled to return one member in 1556, when the Mayor, two bailiffs, and nine aldermen were the entire constituency. Afterwards all householders not receiving alms were added to the electorate. In monastic days, the mitred Abbot of Abingdon was a Lord of Parliament. Oliver Hyde, a merchant clothier, was the first member for the borough, and the sitting representative, Mr. J. C. Clarke, has been engaged in the same important industry. There are now 914 voters on the register. Mr. T. Duffield, who ran away with the daughter of Elwes, the miser-M.P., represented this borough for several years, and was followed by Sir F. Thesiger, Attorney-General under Lord Derby, and afterwards (as first Baron Chelmsford) twice Lord Chancellor.

Clitheroe first returned two members in 1558, but the Reform Act struck off one when it added the £10 householders to the franchise. Prior to this the constituency consisted of the tenants for life or in fee of certain borough lands and houses. The Duke of Buccleuch long enjoyed chief local influence here. There are now some 2060 electors, who are represented by Mr. R. Fort. His father was member for the borough, as was also Lord Cardwell.

Tamworth has returned two members since 1563, its constituency originally being formed of the scot-and-lot inhabitants. The burgess roll now contains the names of 2311 voters. At the last general election Mr. H. A. Bass and Mr. J. S. Balfour were elected members for the borough. The Peel and Townshend families have shared the Parliamentary patronage of

Tamworth, many members of both having owed their seats to the local influence thus possessed. The name of the great Sir Robert Peel appears on the list of representatives. Addressing the voters at an election dinner in 1837 he gave them some memorable advice. Sir Robert said: "It may be disagreeable, and, indeed, inconvenient, to attend to the registration of voters which annually takes place throughout the country; but you may depend upon it, it is better you should take that trouble than that you should allow the Constitution to become the victim of false friends. The advice which has been given by some persons was, 'Agitate, agitate, agitate!' The advice which I give you is this—Register, register, register!"

Retford, Cirencester, Eye, and Woodstock all first returned two members in 1571. The two latter had their representation reduced by one-half at the passing of the first Reform Bill. Mr. Ashmead-Bartlett was returned at the general election to represent the little constituency of 988 voters, which prior to 1832 was very much smaller, comprising only the scot-and-lot inhabitants. The Kerrison family were paramount here for a lengthy period, and the first and second baronets were both members for the borough, as was Sir W. (afterwards Lord) Gifford, Judge Garrow, the first Lord Cowley, the great Marquis Cornwallis, and Sir Joseph Jekyll. Woodstock originally had an electorate formed from the Corporation and freemen. The Duke of Marlborough's nominee has for many years sat for the borough, and it is scarcely necessary to mention that Lord Randolph Churchill is the present member. Besides the Churchills who have represented the pocket borough of Blenheim, the present Earl of Shaftesbury, the Earl of Auckland, and Lord Colchester (as Mr. Speaker Abbot) are among noteworthy members for Woodstock. Cirencester, which lost its second member in 1867, returned Mr. T. W. C. Master without opposition as its representative at the general election. The house of Bathhurst has greatly governed the Parliamentary history. There are now 1138 electors, but before the Reform Bill of 1832 the householders within the old borough limits only were on the burgess roll. Earl Bathurst was member from 1857 to his succession to the title in 1878. Others of this eminent house have sat for Cirencester, including the Lord Chancellor who was elevated to the earldom, and Allen Bathurst, Sir Robert Walpole's political opponent. Cirencester sent representatives to the great Council of Edward III., held in the eleventh year of the reign, but the regular representation dates only from 1571. East Retford has managed to maintain its dual representation until the present day, although it narrowly escaped disfranchisement (along with Penryn) in 1828, in consequence of bribery and corruption, and in order to provide for the enlargement of the representation of Manchester and Birmingham. The ancient constituency was made up of the freemen by birth and service. Oldfield says of the famous Retford King's Bench case in 1802, "It appeared to have been the custom for two hundred and twenty years for the sheriffs and aldermen to make whom they pleased freemen, for the purpose of creating voters, till they became so confident of their possessing such a power that they proceeded to create forty-two honorary freemen at one time. This caused an information in the nature of a *quo warranto* to be filed, within six years, as the statute limits such information to that period after they obtain the freedom of any Corporation." The Corporation pleaded old custom; but the Court replied that it had also been customary to rob on the highway for many years, but that the offender was always hanged upon detection. Judgment of *ouster* was decreed against the whole forty-two honorary freemen. Retford was somewhat purged in 1829, after its Parliamentary life was saved by the electorate being altered to include inhabitants of East Retford and the freeholders of the hundred of Bassetlaw. The old constituency was, like Cirencester, called on to send representatives anterior to the borough having a permanent place on the roll of Parliament. There are now 8434 electors, Messrs. Mapping and Foljambe being returned at the last general election.

The little Yorkshire borough of Richmond, with an electorate only now numbering 721, has been for a long time under the undisputed sway of the Dundas family; and a brother of Lord Zetland, the Hon. J. C. Dundas, is the sitting member. Richmond had double membership from 1585 to 1867, when one was taken away. The ancient burgesses were the old electorate. The most illustrious member Richmond ever returned was the present Lord Chancellor. Newport, Isle of Wight, began its Parliamentary life at the same time as Richmond, and was deprived of its second representative by the same Reform Act as the northern borough; and both are doomed to die together. Newport had a voters' list confined to the corporation of freemen, a small body taken altogether in old days, but now there are 1315 burgesses, represented by Mr. Charles Clifford. Lord Palmerston's first seat was for Newport, he being returned with the Duke of Wellington in 1807. The chief local influence was formerly in the hands of the Worsley family and the Holmeses. Lord Palmerston, in his autobiography, says, respecting his return, "I came into Parliament for Newtown, in the Isle of Wight, a borough of Sir Leonard Holmes'. One condition required was that I should never, even for the election, set foot in the place, so jealous was the patron lest any attempt should be made to get a new interest in the place." Canning similarly owed his first seat to this constituency, it being procured for him by Pitt, as Canning himself said, without a farthing of expense, though Pitt was the poorer man. The first and second Lords Melbourne also sat for Newport. In the pension list of Charles II. (writes Oldfield) the following paragraph appeared:—"Sir John Holmes, Sir Robert's brother, and member for Newton, a cowardly, baffled sea-captain, twice boxed and once whipped with a dog-whip, was chosen in the night without the head officer of the town, and but one burgess present, yet voted this last election, and will be re-elected."

SOME SEVENTEENTH-CENTURY BOROUGHS

The charter of incorporation of Bewdley has been subject to numerous changes. The original deed, renewed by James I., was surrendered to the second Charles, and replaced by another from his successor which last, on the accession of Anne, was declared illegal. This caused much contention, and produced a lengthy law-suit, ending in the confirmation of the original charter. By virtue of this the Corporation of Bewdley, consisting of a bailiff, a recorder, a high-steward, and twelve capital burgesses, were called on to depute one member to Parliament, the bailiff being returning officer. The Reform Act of 1832 added the £10 householders of the borough and an outlying district, and now the voters number 1276. Mr. Harrison was returned at the general election, but was unseated on petition, and at the new election in July, 1880, Mr. E. Baldwin, the iron-founder, was chosen for the vacant seat. The local influence was long divided between the Lyttleton and Winnington families. Tewkesbury first regularly returned two members in 1610, and continued so to do until 1867, when one was withdrawn. The freemen and freeholders were the voting body before the first Reform Bill, and now the burgesses number 748 out of a population of 5100. Mr. W. E. Price, returned at the last general election, was shortly afterwards unseated on petition, and his place taken by Mr. R. B. Martin, who had previously contested East Worcestershire and the City of London without success. He, like Mr. John Martin, who was returned in 1857, is a banker. Mr. Hanbury Tracy (afterwards Lord Sudley) and Mr. Humphrey Brown (of British Bank celebrity), as well as the first Earl of Shaftesbury, who was elected Lord Chancellor in 1672, are noteworthy members for Tewkesbury. Tiverton was enfranchised by the first James in 1615, and has had two members ever since, though there are now only 1414 voters. Sir J. H. Amory and the Right Hon. W. N. Massey were the successful candidates in 1880, and on the latter's death at the end of the following year, Viscount Ebrington was elected. The old Corporation was the electorate prior to the extension of the franchise. The Earl of Harrowby was formerly the patron of the borough, and after the decadence of his political power, the chief local influence passed into the hands of Mr. Heathcoat, the lace manufacturer. As early as 1782 we find the inhabitants petitioning Parliament for popular representation, and pointing out the anomaly of a Corporation of 24 choosing two members (many of the voters being non-residents). Dissent in religious matters has taken sturdy foothold here, and not a few independent-spirited Radicals have made themselves heard in the electoral life of the borough. Lord Palmerston was long member for Tiverton. At the general election in 1852, his return was unopposed, but he had to submit to a running fire of questions from some of the Radical electors, and especially from a persistent local politician named Rowcliff, a butcher of the borough. Lord Palmerston, [illegible] the course of his reply to this troublesome burgess, said: "My good friend, Mr. Rowcliff, has reproached me for not coming often enough among you. I must say that he does not appear disposed to make my visits here particularly agreeable to me. (Laughter.) . . . Mr. Rowcliff says that I only told you of the good that Governments and Parliaments have done, and that I have myself done, and that I have not told you of the bad. Why, God bless me! it was quite unnecessary for me to do that when he was here. (Loud laughter.) If there was a bad thing to be recorded, to be invented, or to be imagined, I am quite sure Mr. Rowcliff would be the first man to tell you of it. (Laughter, which was increased when Mr. Rowcliff called out 'Question!') Well, Mr. Rowcliff is impatient under this castigation. I will hit lower or higher, just as he pleases, but he must allow me to hit somewhere. Mr. Rowcliff has asked me what government I mean to join. Now, that is a question which must depend upon the future; but I will tell him what government I do not mean to join. I can assure you and him that I never will join a government called a Rowcliff Administration." The noble lord presently touched as follows upon another question that had been put to him: "I am for septennial Parliaments. A septennial Parliament, practically, is not a Parliament that lasts for seven years, for we all know that the average duration of the Parliament during the last thirty or forty years has not been more than three or four years. If you establish annual Parliaments you will have the country in a perpetual commotion. Your members of Parliament will not have time to learn their duties, and your business will be ill done. In the same way, if you have triennial Parliaments, during the first year the members will be learning their business, in the second year they will just be beginning useful measures, and in the third year they will be thinking of the Rowcliffs of their respective constituencies — (laughter) — and endeavouring to shape their course, not for the good of their country, but in order to conciliate the most noisy of their constituents." During the last century Tiverton numbered among its members the Earl of Sunderland and Sir Dudley Ryder. Harwich first returned two members in 1615, with a single earlier exception, and lost one in 1867. The old borough voters consisted of the Corporation and capital burgesses resident in Harwich and Dovercourt, and, after the passing of the Reform Bill, the patronage of the representation was largely in the hands of the Government of the day. Among the eminent men returned for the borough we find the names of Right Hon. V. C. Townshend, Lord Liverpool, Huskisson, Canning, Vansittart (afterwards Lord Bexley), and the Right Hon. J. C. Herries. Thomas King, who had been member for Harwich, obtained in 1681 from the Lord Chancellor a writ *de expensis burgensium levandi*, which is the last recorded instance of formal payment of wages to a member. Sir H. W. Tyler obtained a majority of votes at the last general election, the total number of burgesses then being

863. Great Marlow first permanently returned two members in 1624, the scot-and-lot inhabitants being the electors. One was struck off in 1867, and with an electorate of 939 General O. V. C. Williams was chosen representative for the borough in 1880. The Clayton and Williams' families have had the chief political influence. Formerly the borough was coterminous with the parish of Great Marlow; but Little Marlow, Medmenham, and Bisham, across the river, were added by the first Reform Act. Bulstrode Whitelock, Lord Commissioner of the Great Seal, was returned in 1660, and Lord Shelburne in George I.'s reign. Malton had regular representation by two members from 1640 to 1867, and from that period a single member only, Earl Fitzwilliam being paramount in influence there. The New Malton burgage tenants were the old constituency, but that has been enlarged to include the householders of Old Malton, as well as those of the original borough, and there are at present 1374 voters, whose representative is the Hon. C. W. Fitzwilliam. Grattan, Burke, Lord Jeffrey, and other celebrities have been returned members for Malton. Northallerton also dates its continuous dual representation from 1640, but lost its second member in 1832. The Lascelles and Pierse families have been chiefly influential here, and the constituency was originally of similar formation to that of Malton. In 1880, Mr. G. W. Elliot was chosen member for the borough, there being 859 electors. The burgage tenants of Northallerton, record has it, knew how to make the most of their votes in the good old times, and obtaining a seat in the borough was a very costly undertaking. We regret that space will not permit us to enlarge upon the electoral curiosities of the old North Riding town. Newark, which has enjoyed a double membership since 1678, has now 2172 electors in place of the old constituency of scot-and-lot inhabitants. At the general election there was a very close poll declared, the numbers being: T. Earp, 1073; W. N. Nicholson, 993; Hon. M. E. Hatton, 985; S. B. Bristowe, 982. The present Premier was first returned to Parliament, in the Conservative interest, in 1832 for Newark, then under the influence of the Duke of Newcastle. His Grace achieved celebrity for having evicted upwards of a hundred persons who voted against his wishes, and for the following response to a remonstrance: "May I not do as I like with my own?" Lord John Manners also sat for Newark, as did several foregoers in his family, and a number of successive scions of the great house of Pelham-Clinton.

(To be continued.)

THE DYING BOROUGHS.

Episodes from the Parliamentary History of the Towns to be Extinguished by the Redistribution Bill.

By a Fellow of the Royal Historical Society.

XIII.—THE LAST OF THE DOOMED BOROUGHS.

FIVE FIRST REFORM BILL BOROUGHS.

Of the forty-three new boroughs created by the famous first Reform Bill, five are doomed to disfranchisement by the latest measure for the redistribution of seats Macclesfield and Stroud are each two-member constituencies, the remaining three boroughs returning one member each only. Macclesfield, so to speak, is dead already, the writ having been suspended since March, 1881, when the Royal Commission declared the last election void because of the extensive bribery which had been practised in the borough. The Commissioners reported that they were much struck by the open, fearless, and confiding manner in which corruption had been engaged in by both sides, and added that "though it seems doubtful whether a contested election has ever been fought in Macclesfield on really pure principles, the corruption at the late election was far more widespread and far more open than had been the case at any previous Parliamentary election." They scheduled no less than 2872 persons as guilty of corrupt practices, including the two members unseated on petition, Messrs. Brocklehurst and Chadwick, as well as certain justices of the peace, aldermen, and councillors. Almost the entire electorate had, in the opinion of the Commissioners, been operated on by bribery, and numbers of burgesses confessed to having received bribes from both political parties. Each side engaged "money captains," whose business it was to distribute douceurs among the electors in their respective wards. One of the unseated members testified to having taken part in politics since 1832, when his father was returned at the first election for the borough. "He had no doubt there was a good deal of electoral amusement going on at the late election. It had been the custom in Macclesfield since 1832 to distribute refreshment tickets to voters after the election. He could remember standing at the polling-booth presenting voters with tickets in his father's name, giving 6s. for a single vote and 12s. for a plumper. Not infrequently tickets dissolved into drink, and he remembered one woman telling how she and her husband bought a barrel of ale, took it home, sat up with it, and 'rostled' with it till it was finished. Candidates were on happy terms with the voters in those days, and there was a general jollification at elections." Some of the offenders were brought before the Queen's Bench Division for punishment in the November following the sitting of the Bribery Commission, and two solicitors of Macclesfield were sentenced to nine months' imprisonment *without* classification as misdemeanants. The Commission at Macclesfield was a most expensive one; costing over £5000; £1200 was set down for shorthand notes. The Parliamentary history of Stroud presents little of general interest, the most noticeable matter being the connection of Lord John Russell with the borough, which he represented from May, 1835 to 1841, when he was returned for the City of London. Stroud came to his rescue when, on taking office in April of 1835, he lost his seat for South Devon. This remarkable statesman, the "calm Johnny who upset the coach," as Lord Lytton styled him in his "New Timon" (referring to the fall of Earl Grey's Ministry in 1834), was, as all the world knows, the author of that bold Reform Act, the unfolding of the proposals of which so startled politicians in 1831. His life-story is familiar to all. We may take as a specimen of his public utterances an extract from a speech delivered to the electors of Stroud at the election of the new Parliament which followed the accession of her Majesty in 1837. Referring to the suggested abolition of the terms Whig and Tory, and the adoption by the latter party of the then new designation Conservative, Earl Russell said: "If they are really and truly conservatives as regards the general institutions of the country, no name is deserving of more adherents, or would meet with more general approval; but with them it is a mere change of name, a mere *alias* to persons who do not like to be known under their former designation, and who under the name of Conservatives mean to be conservative only of every abuse—of everything that is rotten—of everything that is corrupt. If that, then, is the name that pleases them—if they say that the distinction of Whig and Tory should no longer be kept up—I am ready, in opposition to their name of Conservative, to take the name of Reformer, and to stand by that opposition. And in looking back to history, taking their sense of the denomination of Conservative, I think one may be as proud of the name of Reformer as they can be of the name of Conservative. What was Luther? Luther was a Reformer. Leo the Tenth, who opposed the Reformation, was a Conservative. What was Galileo? Galileo, who made great discoveries in science, was a Reformer. The Inquisition, who put him into prison, was Conservative. So, in the same way, with respect to every part of history, we find that in all times and in all countries there have been Reformers and Conservatives. The Christians who suffered martyrdom in Rome were Reformers. The Emperor who put these Christians to death, Nero, was a Conservative." The chief local political influence was in the hands of the Earl of Ducie, and the third earl sat for Stroud in 1852-3 as Viscount Moreton. On that peer's succession to the earldom the Right Hon. Edward Horsman, Irish Secretary under Lord Palmerston, was chosen to take his place as member for Stroud. At the last general election Mr. W. G. Stanton and the Hon. H. R. Brand, son and heir of Viscount Hampden, the late Speaker, were returned members for Stroud, which has an electorate of 6332 voters. The representation of Frome has, since the borough was added to the roll of Parliament in 1832, been a good deal in the hands of the Boyle family, and the present Earl of Cork and Orrery, head of the house, as also his brother, Colonel the Hon. W. G. Boyle, have been among the representatives. Mr H. B. Samuelson was returned unopposed at the general election; but it is worthy of note, as showing the cost of an uncontested election, that the expenses of his candidature were £379 3s. 5d. Of this £89 12s. was returned as for printing and advertising, £70 17s. 3d. for hire of public halls, committee rooms, &c., and £167 8s. 8d. for professional agency, clerks, postage, messengers, &c. The population of Frome, which was 12,240 in 1832, and had fallen in 1850 to 10,148, is now given as 9376; while the electorate, 322 at the creation of the borough, and 383 in 1857, has been enlarged to a total of 1390. Kendal, created in 1832, a borough with 327 voters, consisting of the £10 householders of Kendal and Kirkland, has now 2108 electors, represented by Mr. James Cropper, who was chosen at the bye-election occasioned by the death of Mr. J. Whitwell, in December, 1880. Mr. George Carr Glyn, the banker, represented Kendal for many years. The principal part of the patronage of the borough was divided between the Tufton and Lowther families. Whitby's short Parliamentary life has been a quiet one. Mr. Arthur Pease, the present member, was first returned in 1880 by a substantial majority. There are 2325 voters on the burgess roll, as against 422 in 1832. Robert Stephenson, of the famous family of railway engineers, who sat for a number of years as representative of Whitby, is the most illustrious of the members of Parliament returned by the romantic Yorkshire seaside borough.

DOOMED BOROUGHS OF SCOTLAND AND IRELAND.

Notwithstanding the union of the crowns of Scotland and England by the accession of James I. to the throne vacated by the death of "good Queen Bess," the country "ayont the Tweed" continued its own separate parliament for upwards of a century, until in 1707, when Anne ruled in Britain the parliament of the North was merged into the assembly at Westminster, though not without strenuous opposition on the part of the Scotch. The system of representative peers was arranged, and forty-five members of the House of Commons, selected by the Scotch constituencies, provided for, two-thirds of these being allocated to counties, and the remainder to the boroughs. In the latter constituencies the electorate, as settled by the first Reform Bill, consisted of the £10 house-occupiers (whether proprietor, tenant, or joint occupier), together with the *bona fide* owners of such properties, resident or not, and husbands, *jure uxoris*, after the death of their wives, holding by the courtesy of Scotland. These were enfranchised in 1832 in lieu of the magistrates and town-councillors, who previously used to choose the representatives. Scotland will only have two of its constituencies struck off by the new Seats Bill—

the Haddington and Wigtown Burghs. The former returned Sir D. Wedderburn at the last general election, and on his resignation in 1882, Mr. A. C. Sellar was selected to succeed to the membership. The burgh district comprises at present some 1805 voters, and a population of 13,755. The Earl of Lauderdale's influence was at one time dominant over the representation here. Among the most noteworthy members have been the Hon. H. Erskine, brother of the Lord Chancellor of that ilk, the second Viscount Melbourne, and General Sir H. R. Ferguson Davie. The Wigton Burghs have 1340 electors in place of 326 in 1832. Formerly the Earls of Galloway and Stair enjoyed between them the chief influence over the representation. In 1880, Mr. J. McLaren (since made a Lord of Session) was returned by a majority of twelve over Mr. M. J. Stewart, his Conservative rival. On Mr. McLaren being appointed to the Lord Advocacy, a new election ensued, when Mr. Stewart turned the tables upon his opponent, defeated him by 23 in a poll of exactly one more than that registered at the general election. A petition against Mr. Stewart's return was presented, however, and that gentleman lost his seat. Another contest ensued, in which the Conservative candidate, Sir John Hay, a distinguished naval officer, and ex-Lord of the Admiralty, was able to hold the seat gained by his party, he obtaining 16 votes more than Mr. G. McMicking, the Liberal candidate. Sir John M'Taggart and Sir William Dunbar may be mentioned among earlier representatives.

The Parliamentary Union with Ireland, which came into effect on the 1st of January, 1801, was carried by the energy and determination of Lord Cornwallis, the Lord Lieutenant, and Lord Castlereagh. The "Correspondence of Charles, First Marquis Cornwallis," published in 1858, reveals the secret measures adopted to effect this important legislative measure. There were 300 members in the Irish House of Commons, 50 of whom were barristers. The large sum of £1,260,000 was spent in the purchase of pocket boroughs from the patrons, about £15,000 being given for each. Lord Downshire received £52,500 for his interest of this kind, and Lord Ely £45,000. Twenty-two Irish peerages were created as bribes, nineteen Irish peers were advanced to higher estate, and five obtained English peerages. Pensions and places innumerable were granted to less influential recipients. The Opposition was almost equally corrupt, and as much as £5000 was given on either side for an individual vote. The Act of Incorporation allowed a hundred members of the House of Commons to Ireland, with twenty-eight temporal and four spiritual peers in the House of Lords. The city and borough constituencies under the Reform Act were made up of the surviving freemen and burgesses who had votes before the bill became law, freeholders of estates acquired before 1832, and occupiers of houses of the annual value of £10, or of lands or houses assessed with the £8 poor rate. Twenty-two Irish constituencies are to be deprived of their members by the new Redistribution Bill, viz., Armagh, Athlone, Bandon, Carlow, Carrickfergus, Clonmel, Coleraine, Downpatrick, Drogheda, Dundalk, Dungarvan, Dungannon, Ennis, Enniskillen, Kinsale, Lisburn, Mallow, New Ross, Portarlington, Tralee, Wexford and Youghall. The city of Armagh, with 634 electors, returned Mr. G. De La P. Beresford, unopposed, at the general election. Athlone chose the late Sir J. G. Ennis at the same time, he receiving 163 votes to Mr. Ed. Sheil's 162. Sir John died in 1884, and Mr. J. H. McCarthy, jun., Nationalist, was returned without opposition in his stead. There are only 344 voters in the borough. Mr. James Talbot (afterwards Lord Talbot de Malahide), the Hon. H. Hancock, John O'Connell, and Mr. W. (afterwards Judge) Keogh, are among former members for Athlone. Bandon, the representation of which has been for many years in the hands of the earl to which the borough gives title, returned Capt. Bernard at the general election by a majority of 15 over Mr. Allman, the Liberal candidate, who, however, succeeded in obtaining the seat in the following June, on the retirement of the captain. There are 398 electors on the roll. As might be expected from a close borough under the rule of the family of Bernard, quite a number of members of that name occur, in addition to whom we may notice Serjeant (afterwards Judge) Jackson. In 1880 Mr. C. Dawson was returned in the Home Rule interest for Carlow, a constituency with 291 burgesses, where at one time the Bruen and Bunbury families were chiefly influential. Mr. W. (afterwards Judge) Maule, and the notorious John Sadlier were members for Carlow. Carrickfergus, with 1420 voters, returned Mr. T. Greer at the last general election. Here the three Marquises of Hertford, Donegal, and Downshire at one time shared the political patronage. Clonmel, which gave Mr. Arthur Moore a seat in 1880, has 432 electors. Judges Ball and Pigott sat for this borough before their elevation to the Bench; and the Bagwell family had chief local inflence at the election of members. Sir H. H. Bruce was chosen at Coleraine at the general election; 462 burgesses have the franchise in this borough, in place of 207 in 1832. The Beresfords were paramount in Coleraine years ago. Downpatrick sent Mr. J. Mulholland to St. Stephen's in 1880 to occupy the seat formerly filled by John Wilson Croker and many of the Kers. In 1832 there were 507 voters registered in this borough, though 299 only enjoy the franchise at the present time; and the population is also considerably less than was the case fifty years ago. Drogheda has 670 electors, who returned Mr. Benj. Whitworth at the commencement of the present Parliament without opposition. Mr. R. Plunkett and Sir W. Somerville, who was in office under Lord Palmerston, sat for Drogheda. Dungannon, with an electorate of 300, chose Mr. T. A. Dickson as its member five years ago, he receiving 128 votes against 126 recorded for the Hon. W. J. Knox, a scion of the family of the Earl of Ranfurly, which swayed the choice of the burgesses at one time, and who had himself for many years represented the borough. A petition was presented against Mr. Dickson's return, and he being in consequence unseated, his son, Mr. J. Dickson, now contested the constituency against the Hon. Mr. Knox. Though the latter secured two votes more than the polling previously taken, Mr. Dickson's total reached 132, and the latter was declared duly elected. His father the following year regained a seat in the House of Commons as member for County Tyrone, *vice* Mr. Litton, who had been chosen a commissioner under the Land Law Act. The hon. and gallant Colonel Knox was again Mr. Dickson's opponent at the poll. Dungarvan has 305 voters, represented by Mr. F. H. O'Donnell. The Duke of Devonshire interest here was large, and in 1832 the burgess roll contained more than double the number of names now registered therein. Richard Lalor Sheil and John Francis Maguire were both members for Dungarvan in their time. Ennis, represented by Mr. M. J. Kenny, has only 253 persons in enjoyment of the franchise. Lord Inchiquin's influence was very considerable in the constituency at one period. Prior to the passing of the Reform Bill, a noticeable name among the members for Ennis was that of Smith O'Brien, and more recently the Right Hon. J. W. Fitzgerald, Irish Attorney-General, sat for the borough. Enniskillen, long a pocket constituency of the earl of the same name, has 452 voters, in whose interest the heir to the earldom was returned to Parliament in 1880. Kinsale has shown a steady decadence for years, both in numbers of population and electors, and there are now 199 names on the burgess roll, Mr. E. Collins, the Home Rule candidate, securing the majority of their suffrages at the general election. Lisburn, chiefly dominated in the past by the influence of the Marquis of Hertford, returned Sir R. Wallace, Bart., unopposed, five years ago, in the Conservative interest. Sir Horace Seymour and Sir J. Emerson Tennant should be mentioned as past members for the borough, which has an electorate of 885 at present. The borough of Mallow, the present member for which, Mr. O'Brien, has succeeded in gaining an unenviable notoriety for his factious action against the institutions of the United Kingdom, has 237 voters, and was for many years represented by Sir D. C. Jephson-Norreys, Bart. Mr. W. O'Brien succeeded Judge Johnson in the representation on his elevation from the Irish Solicitor-Generalship to the Bench. New Ross is represented by Mr. J. E. Redmond, elected without a contest in 1881 on the retirement of Mr. Foley. There are 238 registered electors. The Tottenham and Talbot families have furnished several members for Mallow, and were formerly considered to hold the representation in their hands. Portarlington, with only 138 burgesses, is essentially a soldier's borough. It has been represented by fighting men since long before the Union. The Moira, the Farnham, the Warburton, the Coote, the Dawson-Damer, and the Dunne families have all had soldier-sons in Parliament for it; and the present member, Mr. R. F. Brewster, is a heavy dragoon. His predecessor in the representation (now Lord Castletown of Upper Ossory) was a Life Guardsman. The Seats Bill closes the "Military Parliamentary Borough," and its present silent member will go down to history as the last of a long series of soldier-giants who sat for "the Pale Knuckle in the throttle of Leix." It was once, says a correspondent, proposed to the late brave warrior, Colonel Fred. Burnaby, to stand for Portarlington, his return being sure if he would only consent. It did not take the gallant Guardsman long to give a characteristic reply. "Pshaw!" said he, "there would be no fun in getting in for a one-horse place like that." Tralee, with a list of 371 electors, is represented by Mr. D. O'Donoghue. Two sons of "The Liberator," Maurice and Daniel O'Connell, are among the members for Tralee. Wexford, for which Mr. W. Redmond sits, has 522 voting burgesses, and a population of upwards of 12,000. Youghall, long dominated by the Duke of Devonshire, has a constituency of 252 burgesses, who returned Sir J. N. McKenna in 1865, and again in 1874 and 1880. In all these Irish boroughs, so many of which are to be swept away, there was much trafficking of the vote going on in the "bad old times." "The Civil Correspondence and Memoranda of the Duke of Wellington" during the time when he was Chief Secretary for Ireland lift the veil upon wholesale dealings in corruption carried on in high places, the close constituencies of the Emerald Isle being gambled with as so many counters in the hazard of political chance. There is much of general historical interest in connection with these old Hibernian boroughs, but our space is exhausted.

Paisley & Renfrewshire Gazette.

May 9, 1885.

ND - #0049 - 290722 - C0 - 229/152/4 - PB - 9780331509410 - Gloss Lamination